Are you missing
what matters most?

Visionary Parenting

capture a God-sized vision for your family

by Dr. Rob Rienow

randall house

114 Bush Rd I Nashville, TN 37217
randallhouse.com

Visionary Parenting

© 2009 Rob Rienow

Published by Randall House
114 Bush Road
Nashville, TN 37217

ISBN 9780892655762

Printed in the United States of America

www.randallhouse.com

To my wife, Amy

I am so thankful that God brought us together
for the mission of helping our children get
safely home to their Father in Heaven.

Acknowledgments

All thanks to Jesus Christ for loving me, saving me, and awakening my heart to my ministry at home. The Lord has blessed my life with many who have guided me, shaped me, and helped the ministry of Visionary Parenting to grow.

No one has impacted my heart more than my wife, Amy. Thank for you for loving me so much and for believing in me! God knew I desperately needed a helper, and He created you perfectly for me. Thanks to all my children, RW, Lissy, JD, Laynie, and Milly, who have been so supportive, tolerant, and encouraging of their dad during this journey. I am grateful to my mother who impressed my heart with a love for God and to my father who encouraged me and taught me that it is never too late to turn to God.

A big thank-you to all who helped me put this book, *Visionary Parenting*, down on paper. My stepfather, Jack Herklotz, who loves my mom, was lovingly ruthless with his editorial skills. It was just what I needed. Thanks to my brother Marc and his wife, Jill; to my sister Cathy and her husband, Pete; and to my stepbrother and stepsister, Rick and Debra Gantt. You all helped get this book ready, and more importantly I am thankful for our relationships together.

Thanks to Rob Bugh, my Senior Pastor at Wheaton Bible Church, who has encouraged me to share this message.

God has also used many people to turn my heart to my wife and children. I thank Kirk Weaver, Doug Phillips, Ben Freudenberg, Eric Garcia, Peter Rothermel, and Voddie Baucham. God has used each of you in a unique way in my life.

I am thrilled to partner with the ministry team at Randall House in their commitment to equip parents to impress the hearts of their children with a love for God.

Table of Contents

Introduction

The summer of 2004 was a dark summer. My wife, Amy, and I had been blessed with four children. (We now have five!) I had been serving as a youth minister for over a decade. If you had asked me at that time what my priorities in life were as a Christian man, I would have responded quickly and with conviction, "My first priority in life is my personal relationship with God, followed by my love relationship with my wife. My kids come next, and my fourth priority is my ministry in the church." God, spouse, kids, others. Not only did I preach about this prioritized Christian life, I lived it. If the phone rang and my boss was on the other line with a crisis, and at the same time the other phone rang and Amy was on the line with a crisis, where would I go? How would I respond? I would go home. In a crisis, I would not put my work ahead of my wife.

Over the course of that summer, the Holy Spirit began to press me with a difficult question. "What are your priorities if there is no crisis?" During a normal week, where did I give the best of my heart, passion, energy, leadership, and vision? When I considered my life in light of that question, I did not like what I saw. I preached the Christian life priorities of God, spouse, kids, and others, but in my everyday life, the order was completely backwards: others, kids, Amy, God.

It sounds so horrible to say it this way, but my heart was at my job. When I was at work, I was thinking about work. When I was at home, I was thinking about work. My ministry at church was truly my first love.

This was followed by my relationship with my children. I was not an absent father, physically or emotionally. I tried to spend time with them and connect with them personally. But I had no plan, whatsoever, to pass my faith on to my children. As a youth pastor, I had tremendous strategic plans to pass my faith on to everyone else's children! But with the immortal souls that God had entrusted to my care . . . I was just showing up. I gave them my spiritual leftovers after I poured myself out at work.

My next priority was my marriage to Amy. After I gave my best at work and gave the leftovers to the kids, Amy got what few scraps were left. This is not to say that I did not try to spend time with her and do what I could to help around the house, but my heart was not with her first and foremost. I was seen as a strong spiritual leader at my church, while I was providing virtually no spiritual encouragement for my wife.

Because my life was totally upside down and backwards, I was also far from God . . . and I did not even know it.

It was a dark summer because I had to admit that the life I thought I was living was a mirage. I was not a man who put my ministry to my wife and children first. God brought me to a place of deep brokenness and repentance. I confessed and acknowledged the broken state of my life to God and repented to my wife and children. Then God began to graciously rebuild my family on the firm foundation of His Word and His grand purpose for our lives.

I share this with you because I want you to know that the pages of this book come from a story of brokenness more than a story of success. It was God, through the truth of the Scriptures, who changed my life, my marriage, and my family. Now, five years after the rebuilding began, our family continues to learn, grow, repent, and seek God together.

My hope is that God will use this book, as it points you to His Book, to expand your vision and transform your home. I have become convinced that the Bible is a divinely inspired book that reveals God's truth and His purpose for our lives. My prayer is that through this journey:

- you will capture a biblical vision for the eternal and spiritual purpose of parenting.

the Holy Spirit will inspire you to take an honest look at the current state of your family.

- the Lord will empower you for life-changing action that will transform your family for generations to come.
- by God's grace, all your children, grandchildren, and beyond will get safely home to their Father in Heaven.

No matter what your family looks like today—whether you are expecting your first baby, parenting a house full of kids, or preparing for grandkids—God invites you to become a visionary parent or grandparent.

—*Rob Rienow*

CHAPTER 1

What Is the Point?

A Vision of God's Purpose for Your Family

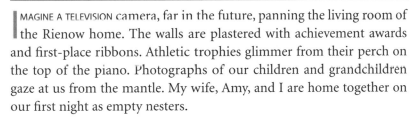

I MAGINE A TELEVISION camera, far in the future, panning the living room of the Rienow home. The walls are plastered with achievement awards and first-place ribbons. Athletic trophies glimmer from their perch on the top of the piano. Photographs of our children and grandchildren gaze at us from the mantle. My wife, Amy, and I are home together on our first night as empty nesters.

"We did it!" I announce. "All the children are smart, athletic, popular, and polite. Our work is done." This scene oozes with the feeling of parenting success at every level.

But is it possible to have all these things and miss what matters most? What if our children and grandchildren do not know God and His plan for their lives?

Sometimes I feel as if just getting through each day is a success. I can get so caught up in what is urgent that I give no attention to what is important. Have you ever stopped to imagine who your children will be when they are twenty years old? What character traits will they have? How will they see the world? What will they believe? Where will they stand with God?

Keep turning the pages of the calendar. Can you picture your children when they are fifty? They will be coming down the homestretch of raising your grandchildren. Will they have taught your grandchildren to love God? Will they be making a difference in their neighborhood for Christ?

Turn some more calendar pages. Consider your sons or daughters at age eighty. You have likely entered the life to come, and they are now grandparents to your great-grandchildren. What sort of legacy will your children have left for their grandchildren? For their world? Will theirs be a story of faith and character? Where will they stand with God?

If we are not intentional with our parenting, we run the risk of ending up with a family filled with achievement, recreation, and niceness. God has a far grander plan for us and for our children. He created our families for a purpose. He gave us children for a reason.

GOD'S GRAND VISION FOR YOUR FAMILY

Now, imagine that you are out shopping and a man comes walking toward you with a video camera and a microphone. He is doing man-on-the-street interviews. The microphone is thrust in your direction and then comes the question, "In your opinion, what is the purpose of family?" There is an awkward pause. Your mind races for something meaningful to say. *Supporting each other. Raising kids. Being a safe place.* After a few moments you blurt out, "Love." Not bad. The man thanks you and moves on to the next person. If that were to happen to you, what would you say?

What really *is* the purpose of family? Why did God choose to give you children? These are questions begging for answers. If we do not know why we are doing something, how can we possibly do it successfully? Thankfully, God has not left us without answers. He is the one who created marriage and family, and He is the one who gave us our children. Since God created family, He is the one who determines its purpose.

Our journey to discover God's vision for our homes begins in Matthew 22:35–38. One of the religious leaders of that day came to Jesus and asked Him a profound question.

> One of them, an expert in the law, tested [Jesus] with this question: "Teacher, which is the greatest commandment in the law?" Jesus replied: "Love the Lord your God with all your heart and with all your soul and with all your mind. This is the first and greatest commandment."

What an important question! Basically he asked Jesus, "If you were to boil down the Scriptures, God's very words to us, into just one thing, what would it be?" Jesus' answer was powerful. There *is* a grand purpose to our lives. According to Jesus, we are created to know and love God with our whole being!

The philosopher Blaise Pascal wrote in his masterpiece *Pensées* that we desperately try to find purpose in everything around us but the "infinite abyss" in our hearts can be filled only by God Himself. We were built by God to be in a deep, personal, love relationship with Him, and if we do not have it, our hearts are restless and our souls ache. Without a relationship with God through Jesus Christ, there is a constant nagging that there *must* be something more to life. There *must* be something to fill the void inside. So we start cramming everything and anything into that void to make it go away. We try money, the latest toys, popularity, sex . . . you name it. The world tells us that if we just grab enough of that stuff and pack it into our lives, we will be satisfied. Sometimes we get what we want and it makes us happy, but only for a short while. Then the ache returns. Jesus, on the other hand, tells us that a love relationship with God is what brings satisfaction to life here on earth and for eternity to come.

THE PRIORITY OF THE HEART

According to Jesus, the most important command in Scripture is to love God. Jesus quoted from the Old Testament, specifically from Deuteronomy 6. Let us go back to the words God inspired Moses to write 1,400 years before Jesus was born. In these verses, not only will we find the commandment from God that Jesus says is the most important in all of Scripture, we will also learn what God wants us to do about it.

> Love the LORD your God with all your heart and with all your soul and with all your strength. These commandments that I give to you today are to be upon your hearts.
>
> DEUTERONOMY 6:5–6

In the verse immediately after the Great Commandment, God reiterates the focus on our hearts. It seems a little redundant. "Love the LORD your God with all your heart . . . these commandments are to be upon your hearts." I believe God knows what our sinful hearts tend to do with religion. We tend to make it all about what we know and what we do. So if we know a lot of Bible information and act like decent people, we feel we are good Christians. Jesus was surrounded by people who knew the Scriptures and sought to follow all the rules (and then some). They were called Pharisees. Jesus confronted them over and over again. Why? Because their hearts were far from God. Please do not think I am minimizing the importance of knowing God's Word and believing His truth. Nor am I saying that our obedience to the Scriptures is not necessary. The point is God knows that if He has our hearts He will get everything else!

More than anything else, God wants your heart and the hearts of your children.

THE SHAPING OF OUR HEARTS

If God wants our hearts and the hearts of our children to love Him, how does that happen? How is the human heart shaped? Have you ever wondered why you are the way you are? Why you have the personality traits you have? Where were the deep places of your heart and character formed?

The greatest earthly influence in people's lives is what they experience in the homes where they are raised. Stop and consider for a moment something that your parents did (or did not do) that shaped and influenced your life for the better. This may be more difficult, but now think back to the home where you were raised to an experience that shaped your heart for the worse. No one can compete with the power of a parent to shape the heart of a child! We all still bear the blessings and the curses of the homes we were raised in. God has given parents and grandparents incomparable power and influence over the hearts of their children and grandchildren. This has proven true in my experience as a pastoral counselor. More often than not the conversation frequently returns to the person's relationship with his or her parents.

Imagine a teenage girl walking through the halls at school. A boy walks up to her and with a sneer says, "Wow, are you ugly! No one is ever going to love you." What a horrific thing to say, and a more horrific thing to hear! The girl runs off to the bathroom, where her friends soon join her . . . and then off they go to beat up the boy. Now imagine that same girl going home after school. She comes in the front door and her father looks up at her from his laptop. With a biting tone he says, "Wow, are you ugly! No one is ever going to love you." Do you think there is any difference between these two events for this young lady? No question about it. The boy in the hall at school was certainly nasty and rude, but I am confident that she will never forget the moment those words came out of her father's mouth. Why is this? Her father and the boy said the same horrible things, right? The difference is that the boy at school does not have God-given power over her heart. Her father does! And he used that power to crush her spirit.

As parents we have overwhelming power over the hearts of our children. Can you remember the feeling you had when you held your newborn baby for the first time? I remember the beautiful moment of holding our fifth child, Milly. She was only minutes old, and I was so aware of how fragile her life was. With one slip of my hand she could fall and be seriously hurt!

As our children grow up, our physical power over them decreases. Pretty soon they are taller and stronger than we are. Our oldest son is just about to pass his mom in height, and he cannot wait! What we fail to realize is that in the same way that we hold in our hands their fragile bodies when they are born, we also hold in our hands their fragile hearts. The difference is that our influence over their hearts does not decrease with age. God has ordained parents with unsurpassed, lifelong influence over the hearts of their children.

This influence may be used for great harm, but God desires to use it for the greatest good. No one can compete with your power to bless your children, to build character in their hearts, and to lead them to faith in Jesus Christ! No one else can provide a home for them where they know that Mom and Dad love God, love each other, and love them. Children who grow up in homes like that overwhelmingly feel a powerful sense of safety. They are far less likely to be driven to experiment sexually in order to find acceptance. They find acceptance at home. They rarely seek to escape into drugs and alcohol because if they have pain in their lives and they need to run for help . . . they run home.

Many of you reading this are single dads or single moms. My parents divorced when I was a sophomore in high school, and from that point forward I was raised by a single mom. For many single parents, my mom included, just getting through each day is daunting. Despite the hardships that we faced in those years, I was able to see my mother's love for the Lord, and for my brother and me. I could not see it then, but God was working all of those circumstances together for good. If you have lost a spouse to death or divorce, my prayer is that you will discover the power of God in your family in ways that you never thought possible.

WHERE LOVING GOD BEGINS

Do you want to obey the Great Commandment? Do you want to love God with all your heart, with all your soul, and with all your strength? Where are you going to start? If I were to ask how you are going to obey the Great Commandment tomorrow, what would you say? I imagine that once again there would be an awkward pause. The challenge is that it is an abstract, global commandment. It looks at life from 40,000 feet. So what does following the Great Commandment look like in our everyday lives down at ground level? God is about to show us.

> *Love the LORD your God with all your heart and with all your soul and with all your strength. These commandments that I give you today are to be upon your hearts.*

DEUTERONOMY 6:5–6

Yes, God! I want to love you! Tell me what to do! God answers our plea in the next verse. Here is where He calls us to begin.

> *Impress them on your children.*

DEUTERONOMY 6:7

So what is the first action step for following the Great Commandment, according to God's Word? We begin by impressing the hearts of our children with a love for God! That is our first and greatest calling!

I believe that these five words, "Impress them on your children," teach us that God's primary plan of evangelism and discipleship is from parent to child. That is the order with which God created the world. His primary plan for spreading the good news of Jesus Christ is the family, beginning with the parent-child relationship.

Have you ever wondered why God gave you children? Here is the answer. He entrusted them to you so that you might do all in your power to lead them to know and love Him. He gave you your children so that you would help them get safely home to their Father in Heaven. He has given you the mission of training your children so that not only will they be saved, but they will have the opportunity to bring many others to Heaven with them.

The purpose of parenting and grand-parenting is to impress the hearts of our children with a love for God. Loving and knowing God is the purpose of life, and you are to lead them to it. Imagine if your children inherited a terminal disease from you. Wouldn't you do everything in your power to find a cure for them so that they might live? This is not an imaginary situation. Our kids have inherited from us something much worse than a terminal illness. They have inherited a sinful nature that points them toward an eternity separated from God. Our most important parenting mission is to lead our children to salvation by God's grace, through faith in Jesus Christ.

The statistics are overwhelmingly clear that if we do not lead our children intentionally, passionately, fervently, to know God and love Him while they are in our homes, the likelihood of them giving their lives to Christ later in life is slim. In fact, only 23 percent of all the Christians in the United States became believers after the age of twenty-one.[1] Why is this? It is because God has given the greatest responsibility and power for evangelism to parents.

QUESTIONS FOR REFLECTION

1. What is something that you experienced in your home growing up that impressed your heart for good?

2. What did you experience in your home growing up that impressed your heart in a negative way?

3. If God were completing these statements, what do you think He would say?

    • My desire is that your child will become . . .

    • My desire is that your child will feel . . .

    • My desire is that your child will believe . . .

    • My desire is that your child will choose . . .

ENDNOTES

[1]George Barna, *http://www.barna.org/barna-update/article/5-barna-update/196-evangelism-is-most-effective-among-kids.*

CHAPTER 2

A Discipleship
Center

A Vision for Spiritual Transformation

WHAT IS GOD'S PURPOSE for the family? God created the family to be a discipleship center! He created your family to be a spiritual-transformation center. It is the primary environment where faith and character are formed and shaped. God made your family so that you would help each other to love Him more. You are together so that you might help each other discover Christ together, grow in Him together, and together make a difference in the world for Him.

Up until today, has this been the central passion and purpose of your family? Many families today are recreation centers, activity centers, wealth-building centers, television centers, and anger centers. What kind of "center" has your family been? If you had to fill in the blank, what would you say has been the central purpose and focus of your family?

There is a lot of emphasis in the church today on the importance of discipleship within small groups. Pastors are crying out, "Spiritual growth happens in the context of relationships!" "We have to live in authentic community with one another!" God believes in discipleship small groups too. He just has another name for them. He calls them *families*. The family is the most powerful discipleship "small group" in the world, where "spiritual growth happens in the context of relationships" and where you will find "authentic community" every minute of every day. Are you looking for authenticity? Are you looking for people to "be real"? Just go spend some time in your house; you will find authentic community there . . . for better or for worse.

NOW WHAT?

As God began to impress Deuteronomy 6:7 upon my heart, I was haunted with a question, "What am I *doing* with this responsibility and calling that God has given me to impress the hearts of my children with a love for God?" I was doing a lot to help encourage faith and character in other people's kids at church but hardly anything with my own children. With my spiritual opportunities at work, I was hitting a home run. With my spiritual responsibilities, I was failing miserably. God was now turning my heart to my primary life mission: to impress God's truth and love upon the hearts of my wife and children. But what, specifically, was I supposed to do?

Praise God He does not leave us hanging! He never gives impossible assignments. Nor does He require us to look high and low for our first action step. He gives it to us in the next three verses in Deuteronomy 6.

Love the LORD your God with all your heart and with all your soul and with all your strength. These commandments that I give you today are to be upon your hearts. Impress them on your children.

DEUTERONOMY 6:5–7A

Yes, Lord! I am ready! I want my children to know you and love you! Where do you want me to start?

Talk about them [these inspired words of God] when you sit at home and when you walk along the road, when you lie down and when you get up. Tie them as symbols on your hands and bind them on your foreheads. Write them on the doorframes of your houses and on your gates.

DEUTERONOMY 6:7B–9

So what is the magical, mysterious formula for imperfect moms and dads to help their kids fall in love with God? What is the super secret strategy? Where do we start? *Talk to them!* What a radical, revolutionary concept! God paints a picture of parents who *talk* with their children about spiritual things, and this passage even goes so far as to mention four specific times that are great times to talk to your children about Jesus.

Is it important to be a good spiritual model for your children? Absolutely! We will talk about that in later chapters. Is it helpful to bring them to church? Of course! It is a key commitment of the Christian family. But God's Word speaks clearly to us as parents that our mission to impress the hearts of our kids with a love for God must be rooted in daily conversations and instruction about spiritual things.

FOUR GOD-FILLED MOMENTS

God gives us four specific times that are prime opportunities to reach the hearts of our kids. The first critical time for spiritual training is "when you sit at home." You know, those times each night when everyone in the family is relaxing together, gathered around the dinner table, or just sitting in an unhurried manner, chatting in the living room. What? You mean to tell me that you do not have times like that? You are not alone. Life is moving faster than ever. Few families are ever simply "sitting at home" anymore.

When I first saw this verse I was struck with a terrible feeling. My family was on the fast track of life. We rarely had times when we were sitting together at home, with the exception of meals, and those few times were not filled with spiritual discussion. As I wrestled with this simple instruction from God to talk about His Word with my family at home, I told Him in prayer that, because of my schedule, I did not have time for that! God was far more gracious with me than I deserved. I felt God respond to that moronic prayer with a firm but gentle message. "Rob, if your schedule is preventing you from sitting at home and talking about Me with your family, then the schedule you have chosen is causing you to sin." I was being disobedient to the very first action point and responsibility that I had as a parent. Ouch! I had to confess to God that He was right. Then Amy and I began to make changes in our family's schedule so that we could begin following this first instruction to sit at home with the family and talk about the things of God.

You may be saying, "Okay, maybe I can get my family to sit down together. But what do I do then? What will I say? How will it work? This sounds like super-boring family devotions!"

For many centuries this priority of spending spiritual time together in the home has been called "family worship." In a later chapter we will dig deeper into the importance of family worship and will talk about practical ways to make it engaging, meaningful, and even fun for everyone in the family.

The first key moment for spiritual conversation is when we "sit at home." The text then goes on to give us the second key moment to talk about spiritual things with our kids: "when you walk along the road." In ancient times when you needed to get somewhere you walked. This refers to our transition times, our in between times. God's Word says that these are prime moments to talk to our children about spiritual things, about who God is and what it means to follow Him. So in my family, we are trying to develop the habit of setting aside a few moments to be spiritually focused each time we get in the car. Perhaps it is a prayer for the safety of our trip. Perhaps it is quick review of a Bible passage we talked about in the morning. My goal is to be obedient to this simple command from God.

One morning the family was driving me to work. We were one minute away from church and I had forgotten to have our "car talk," so I quickly said, "Kids, here is one of Daddy's favorite verses from the Bible, Philippians 2:5: 'Your attitude should be the same as that of Christ Jesus.' What kind of attitude did Jesus have?"

They replied simply, "A good one."

I said, "Yes, a good one. (I guess I was expecting something more profound!) He was joyful. He was patient. So as we go through our day, let's remember that our attitudes should be the same as that of Christ Jesus. I love you. Have a good day." It was just a short spiritual touch, tagged onto the last minute of our car ride.

At the end of the day, my wife picked me up and we drove to a friend's house for dinner. Amy and I were having an "honest and open marital interaction" (otherwise known as an argument) in the front seat of the car. Our voices were raised, and things were going in the wrong direction. From the back of the car our seven-year-old called out, "Remember our verse!" That was not what I wanted to hear in that moment, because I wanted to win the argument. Even short spiritual touches can make a difference in the lives of our children. In this case, the verse came back to haunt me as my child confronted my bad behavior. So be careful! If you start investing faith and character in your child it might just rub off on you too.

The third and fourth key times to talk with our kids about faith are "when you rise up, and when you lie down." In other words, the first few moments of the day and the last few moments of the day carry great potential as times to touch the hearts of our kids.

Imagine the impact on your children if the first words they heard from you each morning pointed them toward Christ! It may be as simple as, "Good morning. God loves you!" Even if you are in a hurry, have someone pray out loud for breakfast and specifically ask the Lord to lead you in the day ahead. Unfortunately, mornings can often be filled with stress and conflict. To make matters worse, I am not a morning person. It is easy for me to get up and move immediately into my to-do list rather than spend time with God in prayer and Bible reading. Some days it seems like we all get up on the wrong side of the bed. On those mornings, Amy or I will often suggest that we "start again." We each take some time to be alone and ask God to help us live for Him that day.

Have you ever noticed that some of your best conversations with your kids happen around bedtime? It is not an accident. God told us in His Word that this was a special moment for deepening our heart connection with our children. Try not to rush it! Do not just end the day with, "Okay, off to bed!" Slow down. Sit down on the bed next to your sons or daughters. Let them hear you pray out loud for them. Invite them to pray as well. Ask them if there is anything they would like to talk about before they go to sleep. You never know what windows of opportunity God will open.

Which of these four God-given, power-packed moments would be the place for you to start increasing your spiritual life with your children?

a. Sitting at home together / family worship.

b. Transition times / car time.

c. At the start of the day/ morning moments.

d. At the end of the day/ going to bed.

I hope you will not feel overwhelmed by all this. I believe that God wants us to share spiritual life with our children multiple times every day. But the reality in your home may be that it has been months since you prayed with your kids and even longer since you read the Bible together. Do not be discouraged! The past is the past. You cannot go back but you can go forward. God has a new future for you and your family. Take a moment and pray right now and ask God where He would have you start. Which of these four power moments of the day would God have you give special attention to this coming month? Choose one. Start small. Build a new habit.

BE PREPARED FOR BATTLE

Based on Deuteronomy 6, I am convinced that regular, daily conversations are vital for leading and loving our children to God. For this reason, Satan will marshal his forces against us to keep it from happening. This is why we sometimes feel silly or awkward when we try to start spiritual conversations with our children. The enemy loves it when he can get our hearts more concerned about feeling embarrassed than about connecting spiritually with our kids. He tries to get us to be more passionate about our jobs or our interest in sports than about the souls of our children. He loves it when we buy the lie that our exercise plan is so critical we cannot miss a day, but we can let a month pass without talking to our children about God and His Word. Satan knows exactly what he is doing. God's primary plan of evangelism and discipleship is from parent to child, so that is where Satan attacks!

You may feel that this calling, this responsibility for spiritual parenting, is way out of your league. Let me encourage you. God never calls us to do something and then abandons us when we seek to be obedient. He never sends us into battle without weapons.

START WITH THE HEART

Do you want to become a visionary parent? It starts in your heart. It starts by capturing God's grand vision for your family and by turning your heart to your children. This was God's final call in the last chapter of the Old Testament. In the last words of that era of revelation, God wanted to be sure that parents got the message. The book of Malachi, written in 400 BC, closes with these important words:

> *Remember the law of my servant Moses, the decrees and laws I gave him at Horeb for all Israel. See, I will send you the prophet Elijah before that great and dreadful day of the LORD comes. He will turn the hearts of the fathers to their children, and the hearts of the children to their fathers; or else I will come and strike the land with a curse.*

MALACHI 4:4–6

The Old Testament is punctuated with this prophecy that the day is coming when the hearts of fathers will be turned to their children, and the hearts of children will be turned to their fathers. The last sentence is a bit harsh. God says that if this does not happen, He will strike the land with a curse. What is going on here? In this Scripture we find a principle that runs throughout the Bible. As the man goes, so goes the marriage. As the marriage goes, so goes the family. As the family goes, so goes the church. And as the church goes, so goes the nation. What happens in our homes dramatically affects our churches, our communities, and our nation! Here in Malachi 4, God tells us that if the hearts of fathers are not turned toward their children, then the entire system of God's blessing is disrupted.

The final words of the Old Testament call parents to turn their hearts to their children and, believe it or not, the first words of revelation in the New Testament say the same thing. The era of the New Testament begins when God sends the angel Gabriel to a man named Zechariah to tell him about the son who would soon be born to him and his wife, Elizabeth.[1] We know his son as John the Baptist. Here is what the angel said to Zechariah about his son in Luke 1:17.

> *And he [John] will go on before the Lord, in the spirit and power of Elijah, to turn the hearts of the fathers to their children and the disobedient to the wisdom of the righteous—to make ready a people prepared for the Lord.*

Do you want the hearts of your children to be prepared for the Lord? Turn your heart to them! Ask God to make it the passion and mission of your life to impress their hearts with a love for God and to help them get safely home to their Father in Heaven! When I stand before God someday, I do not believe He is going to judge me on how much money I made. He will not be concerned about how physically fit I was or how well I did on the projects around the house. According to Deuteronomy 6, His first order of business will be to look at what I did with the immortal souls He entrusted to me and Amy.

The idea of visionary parenting may be new for you. It may feel overwhelming and impossible. But be encouraged. You are an unusual parent! How do I know this? Because you are taking the time to actually read a book on parenting. Many of us have parenting books decorating the shelves at home but the bindings have never been cracked. Perhaps a friend or spouse has given you this book to read. Perhaps you are facing significant challenges with your children and you are desperate for help and encouragement. Some of you may be expecting your first child soon, and you are eager to get prepared. I want you to know that you are not reading these words by accident. God Himself has brought you here. My prayer is that as you take this journey down the path of visionary parenting, the Lord will transform your family in ways you never imagined!

God was so gracious to give me a second chance as a husband and a father to become a visionary parent. As I repented and asked Him to change my heart, He changed my marriage and my family! It is never too late. Your children may all be grown and out of your home, but it is never too late for God to use you to encourage faith in their hearts. Are there magic formulas for impressing the hearts of our children with a love for God? Of course not! There are no guarantees. Each one of our children will need to make a personal decision about God. No one can influence that decision more than you. God created specifically for this purpose – to help your children get safely home to Him.

The apostle John writes in 3 John 4, "I have no greater joy than to hear that my children are walking in the truth." Wouldn't you like to be able to shout that from the rooftops when your time on this earth comes to an end? That is what Amy and I want more than anything.

QUESTIONS FOR REFLECTION

1. What are you currently doing to intentionally impress the hearts of your children with a love for God?

2. How does the enemy seek to distract or derail you from your primary mission of building faith and character in your kids?

3. In what ways do you think your parenting would be different if God increasingly "turned your heart to your children?"

ENDNOTES
[1]Gabriel speaking to Zechariah, as recorded in the first chapter of Luke, is the first chronological event of the New Testament.

CHAPTER 3

A Thousand Generations

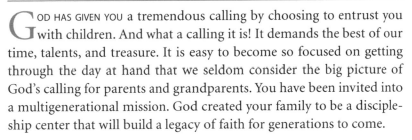

A Vision for Multigenerational Faithfulness

G OD HAS GIVEN YOU a tremendous calling by choosing to entrust you with children. And what a calling it is! It demands the best of our time, talents, and treasure. It is easy to become so focused on getting through the day at hand that we seldom consider the big picture of God's calling for parents and grandparents. You have been invited into a multigenerational mission. God created your family to be a discipleship center that will build a legacy of faith for generations to come.

Once we catch this vision for multigenerational faithfulness, we understand that the parenting choices we make today have the power to affect our children, our grandchildren, our great-grandchildren, and beyond. In this chapter we will learn how to think, strategize, talk, and act in ways that will intentionally cultivate a love for God in the hearts of people who have yet to be born. However, I need to warn you that the four biblical principles we are going to uncover go against the grain of modern and secular views of family life. I hope it comes as no surprise to you that if you want your family to shine for Christ you must be willing to be different from the world. Your goal will not be to blend in with the culture around you, but to transform it.

1. GENERATIONAL CONNECTION MATTERS TO GOD

The extended family, in God's plan, is supposed to be connected. The lines of influence from one generation to the other are supposed to be clear and strong. In our modern culture this is all but lost. Through the combined impact of the industrial revolution taking men out of homes and communities, the entry of women into the workplace in the twentieth century, and the advent of modern transportation, we have become a transitional society.

Even the last thirty years have brought massive changes to the family unit. Many of us grew up in a neighborhood with people we knew and people who knew us. I knew every one of the twenty families on our street where I grew up. We were not close friends with all of them, but at age ten I could tell you the name of every family on the block and knew them at least well enough to greet them. How many of us live in a neighborhood like that now?

Life has certainly changed. Many of us barely know the people next door. Society is more mobile now and more disconnected. Not only have we lost the traditional neighborhood, but we have often lost the extended family as well.

We see the effects of this fragmentation in our culture and in the upcoming generation. People crave connection. Www.ellisisland.org, a genealogy website where you can find the connections to your family history, had 12 billion hits from 2001 to 2008.[1] God built the family to be connected. When it is not, something inside of us longs for it.

Disconnection in the Church

Many churches today are lamenting how the generations within the church are segregated from one another into their "life-stage" ministries. The teens meet with the teens. The senior adults meet with the senior adults. The singles meet with the singles. In some cases, church leaders respond by initiating some multigenerational programming. These new program initiatives are good, and they can have a positive effect on the church community. However, the church programs are not the problem, and therefore they are not the solution. Our local churches are simply reflecting the generational disconnection of our families. Teens are frequently not close to their own grandparents, so can we really expect them to build meaningful relationships with senior adults in their churches? If we want to see multigenerational relationships thrive in the church, we must begin by calling families to live with multigenerational relationships at home.

Generational Connection in the Bible

The Bible underscores this vision of multigenerational connection beginning with Genesis 5, where we the first of many geneologies. Genealogies are not very exciting to read. So-and-so lived this long, and he was the father of so-and-so, and he lived this long, etc. When you do your personal Bible reading, you probably do not spend a great deal of time reading genealogies. In fact, when I am reading my Bible and I come across one, I sometimes skip it and move on to the "good stuff." But, if every word in Scripture is inspired by God, then the genealogies found throughout the Bible must be important. We have to consider why God included them.

All the genealogies that we find throughout the Old Testament and at the beginning of the Gospels of Matthew and Luke tell us about something God values highly. They emphasize the power of the connection between generations and of God's plan to advance His Kingdom through the generations.

You are not alone in this world. You were never meant to be alone. Faith is supposed to come to us through a long line of men and women who know God and love Him. Sadly, few of us have a heritage like that. Some of you are first-generation Christians. Your parents gave you no positive spiritual legacy. For some of you, your parents were the first in the family to come to Christ. That is my situation.

My journey with Jesus began when I was just three months old. My mom was thirty-two years old at the time and was in her second failing marriage. She came to the point where she did not want to live any more. In fact, she was so despondent and irrational that she was thinking of putting me and my brother in a car and driving us off a cliff. But God had other plans. One day in the depths of despair, she called a friend, who immediately came to the house and shared with her the Good News of God's offer of salvation through Jesus Christ. My mom responded to God's grace and put her full faith and trust in Christ for the forgiveness of her sins, and her life changed! From that day forward, she did all she could to impress my heart with a love for God.

My father, then fifty-four years old, was not a believer; in fact, he was actively opposed to spiritual things. It created great tension in my parents' marriage. When I was a sophomore in high school they divorced.

It was a time of deep pain in my life, but the divorce was only the tip of the iceberg as we discovered that my father had been unfaithful to my mother. I was devastated. (I will share more about my father's part in my life story in a later chapter.)

I wish I had been blessed with a long legacy of Christian parents, grandparents, and great-grandparents. Instead, I am the first generation of Christian fathers in my family tree. Perhaps you come from a long line of believers. Your call is to take the torch of faith that has been passed to you from your parents and grandparents, and pass it on to your children and grandchildren. Maybe, like me, you are one of the first Christians in your family. What an opportunity God has given you to launch and build a family that will increasingly impact this world for Christ and His Kingdom for generations to come! Multigenerational faithfulness has to start somewhere!

2. GENERATIONAL CONNECTION IS A POWERFUL INFLUENCE IN CREATING FAITH IN CHILDREN

Abraham was on an adventure of faith—a multigenerational adventure. This adventure of faith was not simply for him, just as your faith is not simply for you. Faith is not just "a personal thing" as so many people like to say. God did not design it that way. God designed faith to be infectious, to spread, primarily and most powerfully, through the family tree, from parent to child, to grandchild, to great-grandchild.

When you think of Abraham and God's plan for his life, do you think big or small? In Genesis we discover that God's plan was to use Abraham and his descendents to be a blessing to the *entire world* and to bring the Good News of God to everyone. God chose Abraham to start a worldwide movement of faith and blessing. So what was Abraham, as an individual man, supposed to do with a calling of that magnitude? Genesis 18:18–19 tells us.

> *Abraham will surely become a great and powerful nation, and all nations on earth will be blessed through him. For I have chosen him, so that he will direct his children and his household after him to keep the way of the LORD by doing what is right and just, so that the LORD will bring about for Abraham what he has promised him.*

In verse 18 we find the big picture of what God called Abraham to do. God wanted all nations on earth to be blessed through him! In verse 19 we find what God wanted Abraham to do as an individual to make the plan happen. His task was to "direct his children and his household after him to keep the way of the Lord." His task was to pastor his children and his household. His task was to teach them about the Lord and nurture faith in their hearts. God said that if Abraham would do this, if he would make it his top earthly priority to lead his family in faithfulness, "the Lord would bring about for Abraham what He had promised him.

Bible-Talk

Did you know that we find the phrases "the God of Abraham," "the God of Isaac," or "the God of Jacob" a total of thirty-two times in the Bible? In addition, there are twenty-one places where we find the phrase, "the God of your fathers."[2]

If a subject of theological importance is in the Bible fifty-three times it means God is trying to say something! I confess that when I see phrases like these in the Scripture, I tend to skip over them. They sound like "Bible-talk." These are just old-fashioned ways of referring to God, right? Yes and no.

In Genesis 26:24, God speaks to Isaac and says, "I am the God of your father Abraham." Why would God speak to Isaac like that? Why would He introduce Himself like that? Because God knows that generational connection is a powerful influence in creating faith in children.

We can imagine Isaac speaking to Jacob and saying, "Let me tell you about the God of your grandfather Abraham," and then going on to teach him about who God is and what God has done.

How many of us have ever talked like that with our kids? For those of you with Christian parents, when was the last time you said to your child, "Let me tell you about the God of your grandmother." We generally do not talk like that. For the men and women of the Bible, it was a normal, regular topic of conversation to talk about faith in a multigenerational way. Why? Because God has created power in spiritual legacy and multigenerational connection!

A few years ago I started experimenting with this in my home. Each night I bless my children before I put them to bed. I took advantage of that opportunity to start using more biblical, multigenerational language. Occasionally I would say, "Now may the God of your Grandma and your Bop-Bop, and the God of your Nana and your Papa Jack, bless you now as you sleep."

I was amazed to see how their eyes and hearts responded to these words. It was as if their spirits resonated with the faith inheritance they were receiving, knowing that their grandparents loved the one true God! A couple of years ago my uncle (my mother's brother) came to Christ. The night it happened I had my usual time of blessing my children, and I said this same thing again: "Now may the God of your Grandma and your Bop-Bop, and the God of your Nana and Papa Jack, bless . . ."

My daughter Lissy chimed in, "Don't forget the God of Uncle Sonny!" Her heart was gravitating to the power that God put into this calling to multigenerational faithfulness.

What if you do not have a legacy of faith in your family? Do not be discouraged! Hang in there. God has a wonderful plan for you, and we will talk about it at the end of this chapter.

3. OUR PRESENT ACTIONS AS PARENTS HAVE SIGNIFICANT IMPACT ON GENERATIONS TO COME

Have you even been tempted to sin and rationalized the act with the thought that "you are only hurting yourself"? Think twice. If you are a parent, this is never true. To understand this, look at the second of the Ten Commandments mentioned in Exodus 20:4–6.

> *You shall not make for yourself an idol in the form of anything in Heaven above or on the earth beneath or in the waters below. You shall not bow down to them or worship them; for I, the LORD your God, am a jealous God, punishing the children for the sin of the fathers to the third and fourth generation of those who hate me, but showing love to a thousand generations of those who love me and keep my commandments.*

There are two extraordinary spiritual principles at work here. The first one is mentioned at the end of verse 5: "I the LORD your God, am a jealous God [which means I want you all for myself, because that is what you were created for], punishing the children for the sin of the fathers to the third and fourth generation of those who hate me."

The best way to understand this passage is to talk about the issue of generational patterns. Generational patterns are behaviors and character traits that run in family trees.

Divorce runs in family trees. Divorce spreads and multiplies. Why? Because parents pass a spiritual legacy to their children and their grandchildren and that legacy influences them. Unbiblical divorce is rampant in my family tree. Thanks be to God, because of the cross of Jesus Christ, that pattern will now end in my life, and by His grace, Amy and I will leave a legacy of marital fidelity to the generations to come!

Abuse runs in family trees. Psychology will never adequately explain why someone who is abused as a child is likely to become an abuser himself. Psychology plays a part, but at the root this is a picture of how particular sins infect family trees. Destructive legacies and influences like alcoholism, favoritism, and laziness are frequently passed from one generation to another.[3]

We Reap What We Sow

God has set a law in place that we will reap what we sow (Galatians 6:7). If you plant a seed, you do not harvest the fruit the next day. There is always a delay between planting the seed and reaping the fruit. We do not like to think about it, but there are times when we sow sinful choices into our lives and the results appear a generation later. Our children and grandchildren are the ones who may eat the fruit. In Exodus 20:4–6, God says that even grandchildren and great-grandchildren can reap what we sow. Thankfully, God has the power to break those patterns in you and in your children. If this concept makes you feel hopeless and helpless, consider this promise from God.

I, the LORD your God, . . . [show] love to a thousand generations of those who love me and keep my commandments.

EXODUS 20:5–6

A thousand generations! This is a promise smack in the middle of the Ten Commandments from God to you. Will you catch a vision for the fact that God has created you not just so you will impact your children, not just so you will impact your grandchildren, but so that your faith and your legacy will result in God showing love to a thousand generations of your descendents?

Is that a big enough vision for you? The power of sin spreads a few generations, but the power of righteousness knows no bounds. Scripture gives a real life example of this in 1 Kings 15, beginning in verse 1.

> *In the eighteenth year of the reign of Jeroboam son of Nebat, Abijah became king of Judah, and he reigned in Jerusalem three years. His mother's name was Maacah daughter of Abishalom.*

1 KINGS 15:1–2

Here is a quick geneology of this family: David, Solomon, Rehoboam, Abijah. Abijah was David's *great-grandson*.

> *[Abijah] committed all the sins his father [Rehoboam] had done before him; his heart was not fully devoted to the LORD his God, as the heart of David his forefather had been. Nevertheless, for David's sake the LORD his God gave him a lamp in Jerusalem by raising up a son to succeed him and by making Jerusalem strong. For David had done what was right in the eyes of the LORD.*

1 KINGS 15:3–5A

Abijah was not a righteous man. He committed horrible atrocities. Yet, God brought certain blessings into his life. Why? For one reason: the faith of his great-grandfather David. This is a spiritual law that God has built into the power of families and into the power of legacies. God promises that what we do right here and right now in our personal relationship with Him—our obedience to Him and our discipleship of our children—is going to have a direct impact in the lives of our descendents. Parents with a vision for multigenerational faithfulness regularly think about the souls of their great-grandchildren!

4. GENERATIONAL FAITHFULNESS IS BUILT UPON

Honoring Our Parents and Grandparents

It is unusual today to have multiple generations of families living near one another, and even if they live close physically, they are often emotionally and spiritually distant from each other. Earlier, we considered a few of the factors that have influenced this disintegration of the extended family in our modern culture such as transportation and job transitions. But there is a deeper force at work here: Western culture has embraced the values of Darwinian evolution. One of the essential viewpoints of an evolutionary worldview is that the elderly are no longer considered valuable to society. They are not strong, so they cannot work. They are not mentally sharp. They wear odd clothes, and, frankly, sometimes they are embarrassing. Once they become sixty-five years old, and certainly when they become seventy years old, they are irrelevant and should join the rest of the out-of-date people in the retirement community.

While we may not like using such blunt terms, this is increasingly the way society views our senior citizens. Where are the churches, families, and businesses that eagerly look for the wisdom and guidance of those who have weathered the storms of life and followed Jesus through thick and thin? I refuse to believe that it is God's plan for people to go through the blessings and trials of life, to learn through painful experiences, to walk with Jesus and know Him in a passionate and personal way, and just when they get to the point of being able to offer some true wisdom and perspective on life, we tell them their time has passed.

Embracing the Fifth Commandment

In the heart of the Ten Commandments, God gives us the first step toward building a family with a multigenerational vision.

Honor your father and your mother.

EXODUS 20:12

If you look carefully at the Ten Commandments, you will discover that this is the first commandment for human relationships. The first four commandments are vertical, they instruct us about our relationship with God. The final six commandments are horizontal, they show us God's will for human relationships. The fifth commandment, therefore, is the first commandment for earthly relationships. God Himself inscribed the commands into stone. He put them in their order. He chose to put "honor your father and your mother" before "do not murder" and "do not commit adultery." We should take note that God put the command to honor parents first in the list of relational commands.

Not only does it come first, but honoring our parents is a lifelong command. It does not expire at the age of eighteen. Honoring our parents is a prerequisite to honoring God. How can we say that we honor and respect God if we are not seeking to show honor and respect to the parents He created for us? But what do we do if we have parents who are not worthy of honor? What do we do if we really do not want our parents providing direction and input into the lives of our kids?

First of all, honoring our parents does not mean we have to like them. If your parents have been vicious and hurtful to you over the years, you are not going to have warm, fuzzy feelings toward them in your heart. However, you can choose to treat them with dignity and courtesy. Warm feelings are not necessary for being polite.

Honoring our parents also does not require trusting them. If your parents are continually hurtful toward you, you are not commanded to allow yourself and your children to be abused by them. You may have to keep a polite distance. However, even if you do not trust them because of their untrustworthy behavior, you do need to act decently and respectfully toward them. Do all you can to avoid talking negatively about them, especially in front of your children. God chose them as your parents and He commands honor.

For those who feel you were raised by terrible parents, consider this. You had no choice about what kind of home you grew up in. However, you can now choose what kind of home your children grow up in and, through your children, what kind of home your grandchildren will grow up in!

The First Commandment with a Promise

Paul says in Ephesians 6 that the fifth commandment is "the first commandment with a promise."

Honor your father and your mother—which is the first command-
ment with a promise—that it may go well with you and that you
may enjoy long life on the earth.

EPHESIANS 6:2–3

This promise has always bothered me a little. This is God's Word. A promise is a promise. So this means that if a person honors his father and mother, he is going to live a long life. So, if a person dies young, does that mean he did not honor his parents? I am not comfortable with that. Can I really stand up in a pulpit and tell young people that if they honor their parents, God promises they will live a long time? Here is how I solved the problem. When I preached on this passage over the years, I did what I could to generalize it and take the edge off. I would say something like, "If you honor your parents, God will bless you." That sounds good. You cannot argue with that, right?

Unfortunately, I was reducing a promise from God into some sort of general truth or proverb. Recently, God used a sermon from Voddie Baucham to unlock the mystery and power of this Scripture for me.[4] The key in approaching this passage is to understand that the Ten Commandments were not written with an individual mindset but with a communal mindset. These are commands for the faith community not just for individual followers of God. So the promise is *not* that individuals who honor their parents are guaranteed long life on earth, but that if parents will follow God and if the children of the faith community will honor their parents and receive their spiritual heritage . . . then God promises that the people of God, the faith community, the church from a New Testament perspective, will live long in the land!

This is a lock-tight promise from the Creator Himself. It has been rightly said that Christianity is always one generation away from extinction. Do you want to see the church of Jesus Christ grow and fill the earth with worshippers of God? It starts with parents loving and following God, and children honoring their parents by following in their footsteps of faith. I believe that the dark side of this promise is also true. If Christian children do not honor their parents, then the faith community will not live long in the land. We have ample history to prove this point. Look at the spiritual condition of Europe today. A few centuries ago Europe was home to the largest number of dedicated Christians on planet earth. Now, Bible-believing Christians represent less than 2 percent of the population.[5]

How could this happen? The answer is simple. Faith was not passed from parents to children, generation after generation. Christianity literally died off.

Do you want to see the loving, gracious church of Jesus Christ advance in our culture today? Then do all in your power to impress the hearts of your children with a love for God. At the heart of the Great Commission are visionary parents and grandparents who will disciple their children, and children who follow in the footsteps of their godly parents.

Ministry Starts with Family

God has a powerful message in 1 Timothy about the call for Christians to demonstrate their faith first by caring for their family members.

> *Give proper recognition to those widows who are really in need. But if a widow has children or grandchildren, these should learn first of all to put their religion into practice by caring for their own family and so repaying their parents and grandparents, for this is pleasing to God.*

1 TIMOTHY 5:3–4

> *If anyone does not provide for his relatives, and especially for his immediate family, he has denied the faith and is worse than an unbeliever.*

1 TIMOTHY 5:8

Do you want to make a difference in the world? Do you have a desire to serve others and meet needs in your community? Then start at home. In Matthew 22 Jesus reminds us that the second commandment is to "love your neighbor as yourself" (Matthew 22:39). When we consider who is our neighbor, should not members of our own family be the first people who come to mind?

This is another area where we will reap what we sow. If we sow dishonor to our parents, we should prepare to reap dishonor from our children when we are old. Do you want your children to honor you? Start by honoring your parents and grandparents. This is the starting place for multigenerational faithfulness. This principle applies whether you have godly parents and grandparents or ungodly parents and grandparents. God wants you to create a culture of honor in your family for those who are older, because it is this "fifth-commandment culture" that will drive the replication of faith in Jesus Christ down through your generational tree.

Ideas for Cultivating Honor

Place Grandparents at the Places of Honor

When your parents or older members of your family are in your home, seat them in places of honor. At the dinner table, serve them first. Give them verbal honor and recognition. When you pray before your meal consider praying something like, "God we are thankful that Grandpa and Grandma can be with us today. We want to honor them, and we thank You for them."

Ask Believing Grandparents to Share Their Wisdom with Your Children

If your parents are believers, consider creating time and space for them to share their wisdom and their stories with your children. Gather everyone around. Encourage the kids to prepare questions in advance. When we have created these times in our home, we have set up a video camera to capture the words, wisdom, and stories for the generations to come. Would you like to have a recorded record of the stories and wisdom of your parents? Most of us would love that. Your kids would love that, too, and God will bless your effort to intentionally provide it for them. Imagine how honored your parents will feel!

Talk Frequently about a Vision for Multigenerational Faithfulness

If you could listen in to the conversations in the Rienow home, you would hear Amy and I frequently beginning sentences with, "That character trait I just saw in you is going to make you a good father/mother someday." The subject of grandchildren comes up regularly! Why? Because we are praying that God will give our children a passion for their roles in the multigenerational mission to which He has called us.

Of course, little kids do not always track with big vision and lofty rhetoric. On one occasion, Lissy, who was seven years old at the time, explained to us that she was going to start a new craft project. Her plan was to make little ponchos for all of her stuffed animals, and to write the name of each animal on his poncho so he would be "labeled." I told her that I was so impressed with her organizational skills and that those skills were going to help her be a great mom. She was puzzled and asked, "Am I going to label my kids with ponchos?"

As a regular part of our family prayer time together, I will pray, "Lord, please let each one of our children love you more than Mom and I do, know your Word better than Mom and I do, and take your gospel farther than Mom and I can." I want them to know that their Heavenly Father and their earthly father are inviting them into a noble calling for Christ and His Kingdom.

Consider getting a poster board and drawing out your family tree. Talk about the people in your family who have gone before, and the lessons the family should learn from them—both good and bad. At the bottom of the family tree, make open spaces for your children's future children. Will God give each of your children kids of their own? Only He knows, but in our family, we eagerly pray that He will.

Perhaps on your family tree, you are the first person who has come to Christ. Recognize your calling! You have been chosen by God to be the spiritual matriarch or patriarch of an awesome, God-honoring, gospel-advancing family tree. Imagine 100 years from now, a young Christian woman is asked to share the story of how she came to Christ. She begins by saying, "My journey to Christ didn't begin with me. It started with my great-grandmother. She was the first one in our family to respond to God's grace through faith in Jesus. She then raised my grandfather to know the Lord, who in turn raised my father to know the Lord, and my father faithfully passed his faith to me." Wouldn't that be wonderful? If your heart beats a little faster when you imagine that scene, you are capturing this powerful vision of multigenerational faithfulness. In our next chapter, we will turn our attention to what a family with multigenerational vision looks like on a day-to-day basis.

QUESTIONS FOR REFLECTION:

1. Do you currently have an intentional plan to show honor to the elders in your family?

2. To what degree do you see the virtue of honor in your children's hearts toward you, and toward their grandparents?

3. Did God challenge your heart and expand your vision as you read this chapter? Write down what the Lord taught you and consider sharing it with your spouse or a close Christian friend.

ENDNOTES

[1] http://www.ellisisland.org/EIinfo/Annual_Report_2008.pdf

[2] New International Version

[3] Is your family struggling with destructive generational patterns? God has the power to break those patterns and stop them from being passed to your children and grandchildren. "The Bondage Breaker" by Neil Anderson will equip you with a biblical foundation for this spiritual battle.

[4] Voddie Baucham, "The Centrality of the Home for Evangelism and Discipleship," February 2006.

[5] According to research from Greater Europe Mission, www.gemission.org.

CHAPTER 4

The Family
Calendar

A Vision for a God-Filled Daily Life

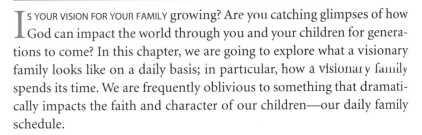

I S YOUR VISION FOR YOUR FAMILY growing? Are you catching glimpses of how God can impact the world through you and your children for generations to come? In this chapter, we are going to explore what a visionary family looks like on a daily basis; in particular, how a visionary family spends its time. We are frequently oblivious to something that dramatically impacts the faith and character of our children—our daily family schedule.

Consider this question. When your sons or daughters leave your home someday, which one of these things would you want most for them?

a) to be successful academically.   c) to be successful socially.

b) to be successful athletically.   d) to be a person of faith
                                          and character.

Personally, I would like to have another option: e) all of the above. But if you could only have one, which one would you choose? You most likely said that faith and character were most important to you. At least that seems like the right answer.

Let me change the question, while leaving the answers more or less the same. Which of the following parenting issues gets the best of your parenting time, effort, money, and planning?

a) academics.   c) social life.

b) athletics.   d) faith and character development.

If you had to rank these four categories in order of the amount of time, money, and effort you put into each one, which would come out on top? Which would come out on the bottom? Five years ago, when God turned my heart to my children, I hated this question. It revealed to me that the thing I claimed was most important to me, the faith and character of my children, was actually at the bottom of my priority list.

Let us imagine that all of our children turn out to be smart, athletic, popular, polite, and hardworking. It would seem that they would be poised for all the success the world has to offer. But what if they do not love God and know His plan for their lives? Most importantly, what if they do not get safely home to Heaven? There is nothing wrong with being great at sports, getting good grades, or being well-liked. The danger is that if these things become our focus, we can completely miss the things that truly matter.

Here is a third and final question. Which of the following receive the most time on your family calendar?

a) academics.   c) social life.

b) athletics.   d) faith and character development.

Once again, when I was faced with this question, I did not like the answer. It seemed as if the family calendar was packed with school events, sports, and activities, with church worship tucked into the appropriate time slots in the week.

THE POWER OF EXPERIENCE

Your children are growing up on all fronts simultaneously. They are growing physically, mentally, emotionally, and spiritually each and every day. For those of you who have little children, you understand that reason simply does not work in some parenting situations. If a child's cognitive abilities are not advanced to the point of being able to filter and evaluate his own experience, reason will be a limited tool in your parenting toolbox. Let us say that a four-year-old boy goes outside to play with his big brother. Another boy in the neighborhood comes up to him and calls him, a "loser." He comes running home crying. You hearken back to some pop-psychology picked up on a talk show and proceed to explain to him that this other little boy is insecure about himself, and that he is projecting that insecurity onto others in an attempt to make himself feel better. How much do you think that reasoned explanation will help your four-year-old? Not much. A four-year-old has not developed reasoning abilities to a sufficient point to be able to filter and evaluate this type of experience. What does a four-year-old boy need who has just been insulted by another child? He needs a hug. He needs to feel that Mom and Dad love him and accept him. He needs to experience love to combat the experience of rejection.

Long before we can reason, our hearts have been shaped by our experiences. Our children are developing their understanding of the world through what they experience at home. This is why our daily family lives and regular family schedules are powerful influences in shaping our children's hearts. In this chapter we will develop four principles to help create a God-filled daily life in your family.

FOUR PRINCIPLES FOR A GOD-FILLED NORMAL LIFE

1: Who We Are at Home Is Who We Really Are

This is scary! The person you are in the privacy of your home is the real you. This is true for all of us. Our true character is always revealed in the real world of family life. Many of us had a parent who portrayed one image outside the home, in the community, but back with the family, when the doors were closed, he or she portrayed a different image.

We do not like to admit it, but the worst part of our character comes out at home. How many people give their boss the "silent treatment"? If you tried that, you would not be his employee for very long. There are consequences to that sort of behavior out there in the fake world of our modern culture, so we reserve that rude behavior for our loved ones.

Imagine that you are a dad and you are invited to a friend's house for a barbecue and pool party. You change your clothes in the bathroom and leave your underwear in the sink. Your friend notices your messiness and says, "Hey, you left your underwear in my sink." To which you snap, "Don't nag me!" Is this how we treat our friends? No. If we did, we would not have any friends at all. Again, this is the sort of insensitivity and defensiveness we reserve for our family members.

Our kids quickly learn how to function in the fake world too. Have you ever had one of your daughter's teachers go on and on about how well she is doing in class, how respectful she is, and how considerate she is of the other students? Of course, we like hearing this type of praise, but in the back of our minds, we are thinking, *Are we talking about my daughter here? Is this the same kid who just threw a complete fit on the way to school this morning because she was not allowed to see her friends after school today?*

We have to control the selfish and immature parts of our character in the artificial world because the consequences can be too immediate and too dramatic. So, we have moms who show great tenderness and patience with the kids they take care of in children's ministry but who are harsh and short-tempered with their husbands and children. Dads are able to stay on top of the details of everything at work but so often seem to forget everything that needs to be done around the house.

At first, it does not seem right that we are at our worst at home. But consider how perfectly God designed the institution of the family. Family relationships are the only relationships hot enough and intense enough to bring out the worst in our character. God created the family in such a way that the worst in us would come out with the very people He made to love us unconditionally and to stick with us for the rest of our lives. What a magnificent plan! Unfortunately, because we do not understand that He created our family as a discipleship center, when those ugly things emerge at home, we strike back with rejection rather than seek to help each other grow.

Living in the Real World

Authentic community is found at home. That is the place where we are the most real and where others are the most real with us. However, our culture teaches us that we will find our purpose and meaning anywhere but at home! The message comes through loud and clear that what really matters is your performance, your work, your fame, and your success. Your private life is just that, private. In the 1990s, we saw this secular line of thinking on full display as the nation responded to the sexually inappropriate actions of President Clinton. While some expressed shock and outrage at his immoral behavior, many others parroted the popular cultural line, "What he does in private does not matter, as long as he is doing a good job as President." That is the opposite message of the truth that who we are at home is who we really are.

This cultural way of thinking creeps into the way we live far more often than we think. Consider the parent who gets a call from the school principal about a discipline situation. The principal explains that the parent's child was disrespectful to his teacher, and talked back to her in front of the class. The parent feels both embarrassment and anger rising inside. The child has also been acting disrespectful at home in recent weeks. When the child comes home later that afternoon, the parent lets him have it. "You may not respect me, but you will respect your teachers!"

Think with me about the underlying message here. What this parents is saying is, "I don't care that much how you act around this house, but if you are out in public, you had better have your act together!" This statement makes perfect sense from a worldly perspective, but from a Christian perspective it is a backward, twisted, and bizarre thought. According to the Scriptures, no one deserves more honor and respect than a child's mother and father! Mom and Dad are ordained by God to receive more respect from a child than anyone else on earth. The command to "honor your father and your mother" is found eight times in the Bible.[1]

Perhaps you are thinking, "I would never tell my son that it is okay to show disrespect to me." You are probably right, but imagine two scenarios. To which of these two events would you react more strongly? Which would garner a greater punishment from you? Scenario one, your daughter, in a fit of anger, gives you the middle finger. Scenario two, your daughter, in a fit of anger, gives her teacher the middle finger in front of the class. Our culture would have us believe that scenario two, the terrible insult to the teacher, is worse because it is in public and what happens in public is what counts. But according to God's Word, there is no comparison between these offenses. Scenario one is the greater offense. I am not saying that this kind of insult to a teacher is not important, but rather that no one deserves more honor than Mom and Dad, and that who your child is at home, is who she really is.

2: A Child's Heart Is Impressed Through His Parents' Character

When I was a youth pastor, most of the students I worked with could not tell me what their fathers did for a living. If they were lucky, they could tell me the name of the company their dad worked for. In rare instances, they knew the general field or job title their dad had. Why is this? Our kids do not care all that much about what we do for work outside the home. They care far more about what takes place in the home and in family relationships. There is not a kid on the planet who would not trade a dad with a high-powered executive position who is never home for a dad with a blue-collar job who loves his wife as Christ loves the church and who gives the best of his time and his heart to his family. Our kids will remember *who we are at home* far more than what we accomplish in our work and activities outside our home.

Can you remember specific things your parents taught you when you were growing up? I am not talking about general principles but about direct quotes. If I gave you a blank sheet of paper, how many direct quotes do you think you could come up with from your mother or father? I think that most of us would be able to come up with a few corny sayings, a couple of jokes, and maybe a snippet of wisdom or two. I doubt we could cover a quarter of the page of paper. But what if I asked you to write down as much as you could about *who* your parents were—their character traits, strengths, and weaknesses? You could fill page after page! Why? Because your heart was deeply impressed by experiencing the character of your parents, and you will remember those things for the rest of your life.

Our kids are impacted by who we are, not just by what we say. In chapter one, we learned from Deuteronomy 6 that God wants us to talk with our kids often about spiritual things. The message here is not in contrast to that teaching but complimentary of it. If you seek to have a God-filled daily life, you will be talking about spiritual things! A godly lifestyle, prayer, and Scriptures will be woven through your daily routines, and your children will observe this. When your children are fifty years old, they may not be able to remember a lot of specific things you said, but if they are asked to describe your character, they will say, "My mom and dad were always talking about the things of God. He was on the forefront of their minds, and that spilled over into everything we did." I pray my children will say that about Amy and me.

3: A Child's View of God Is Formed Through His Parents' Character

The way children view their parents is the starting point for the way they view God. I can remember numerous conversations with teenagers when I asked them to tell me about their dads. To which some would say, "Well he is a good guy, but he is gone a lot. He isn't really much of a talker, so we don't get into real personal stuff." Then I would ask, "Now, tell me how you see God." They would often reply, "I think God is out there somewhere, and I think He is good. But He has a lot going on, so I don't think He is all that concerned about me and my little problems."

Did you see what happened? They transferred their view of their dads to their view of God. They related their experience of the character of their dads to their beliefs about the character of God. Children with parents who abuse them often see God as an abuser. Children with parents who are angry often see God as angry. Thankfully, God's grace can break through every distortion we may believe about Him. The point here is that a child's initial view of God is formed through the character of his parents. This transfer naturally takes place because of how God designed the parent-child relationship. God gave you children so they could see a physical representation of love, protection, patience, kindness, goodness, and forgiveness. When children experience a parent who protects them, their hearts are primed and prepared to believe in a God who protects them. When children experience a parent who forgives them, their hearts are ready to believe in a God who can forgive them. Our character, on display at home, is literally constructing our children's framework for understanding who God is. This is happening in a powerful way through whatever takes place daily in our homes.

4: A Child Learns What Is Important Through the Family Schedule

If someone followed your family around for a full week, observing everything you did and keeping a log of all your activities, what would that person conclude about what is most important to you? If your calendar is the measure of your values and priorities, what does it reveal? Your daily family schedule is actively teaching your kids what you prize most in life.

The movie *Chariots of Fire* tells the true story of Eric Liddel, an Olympic sprinter from Great Britain. Liddel, a devoted Christian, was heading to the 1924 Olympic Games in France when he learned that his race, the 100-meter dash, was scheduled on the Sabbath. He refused to race on the Sabbath despite enormous pressure from the leaders of his country. Liddel made that choice because throughout his childhood his family's schedule prioritized the value, sanctity, and biblical teaching about the Sabbath. He was the best runner in the world and had achieved the honor of participating in the Olympic Games, yet he chose not to race on the Sabbath because of the values he had learned growing up with a God-filled family life. God rewarded his obedience by allowing him to win the gold medal when he ran in a different race later in the week.

Look how far we have come! We are now at the point that if our ten-year-old makes the travel soccer team, everything else in life takes a backseat, including church. We make it to church when we can; if it fits the schedule. My point here is not that missing church is the worst thing in the world. Rather, my concern is that if *every time* sports and church collide on your calendar sports wins, then the schedule you have chosen is teaching your children that you value their bodies more than their souls. Cotton Mather, all the way back in the late 1600s gave parents a powerful challenge. In his book, *The Duty of Parents to Their Children*, he encouraged parents to consider whether they were paying more attention to their children's bodies or to their souls:

> *The souls of your children, must survive their bodies, and are transcendently better and higher and nobler things than their bodies. Are you careful that their bodies may be fed? You should be more careful that their souls may not be starved, or go without the Bread of Life. Are you sure that their bodies are clothed? You should be more sure that their souls may not go naked, or go without garments of righteousness. Do you hate to see their bodies laboring under sickness? You should hate much more to see their souls pining away because of their sins.*

I know many Christians who get on their soapbox when it comes to the busyness of contemporary culture. "We are just too busy these days for relationships." "We are always running at 120 percent, and someday we are going to crash." You have heard this stuff. Perhaps you have made similar statements from your own soapbox. So we all agree that we are too busy. Now what? Where are the families who are actually willing to *do something* about it? They are few and far between. We moan and groan about how frantic life is and then keep right on living like the rest of the world. One of the first steps toward becoming a visionary parent is having the courage to choose a different schedule and a different calendar for your family.

God gives us a great place to start—the Sabbath. For most of my Christian life I completely disregarded the Scriptures about God's will for my time on Sunday.[2] My favorite teaching in the Bible about the Sabbath was directly from Jesus in Mark 2:27: "The Sabbath was made for man, not man for the Sabbath." I never really bothered to study this or search out its meaning using the rest of God's Word as my guide. My unstudied interpretation of Jesus' teaching on the Sabbath here was, "Lots of people have tried to make all sorts and rules and regulations about the Sabbath, but I am here to tell you that you can do whatever you want to do."

Had I thought this through? Of course not. Was I teaching this interpretation to others at my church? No way. This was not a thoughtful searching for truth in the words of Jesus. This was coming from my own desire to do what I wanted, when I wanted to do it. I did not want to deal with any Scripture that might call my agenda into question. Have you ever considered these words of Jesus? Have you ever pondered what He was trying to teach? I believe the best way to interpret a difficult passage in the Bible is by using other Scripture. God never contradicts Himself, and His Word is completely sufficient to teach us everything important about everything important. Consider how God spoke through the prophet Isaiah about how God's people should approach the Sabbath:

> *"If you keep your feet from breaking the Sabbath and from doing as you please on my holy day, if you call the Sabbath a delight and the LORD's holy day honorable, and if you honor it by not going your own way and not doing as you please or speaking idle words then you will find your joy in the LORD, and I will cause you to ride on*

the heights of the land and to feast on the inheritance of your father Jacob." The mouth of the LORD has spoken.

ISAIAH 58:13–14

What is your family's view of the Sabbath? Do you treat Sunday different than the other six days of the week? How might God's words here in Isaiah 58 challenge you to change your family schedule, beginning with this one day each week?

Our family faced our first "sports vs. Sabbath" conflict this past summer. We have always chosen sports activities that do not require practices or games on Sundays. However, our ten-year-old son's baseball team was in the playoffs and had made it all the way to championship day. The game was scheduled for Saturday, but it was pouring rain. The Park District rescheduled the game for Sunday morning at 10 a.m. Ouch! This was a big game, and we had to make a big decision. Our first reaction was to tell our son that he was not going to be allowed to play, but after conversations with several Christian friends who were in the same position, we realized that some families were choosing to go to the early church service and then to the game. This seemed like a good option, but we still felt conflicted. We did not want to make a snap judgment because we know that Christians see this issue differently.

This was a family decision, and we wanted our son's involvement. We read through different Scriptures together, particularly Isaiah 58, as noted above, and Exodus 20:8. His conclusion was stunning. He told me, "Dad, if I play in the game, that will make Sunday feel like any other day, and Sunday is not any other day." With that, he came to the conclusion he was not going to play in the championship game. He asked if we could go over to the game after church to cheer on his teammates. It turned out that his conviction was even stronger than ours. I was very proud of him because he chose to be guided by God's Word.

That Sunday we went to church and then went over to the game, which was about halfway done when we arrived. Our son greeted his team and sat with them on the bench. The players and coaches were enthusiastic about him being there and respected his decision not to play. I even had a dad come up to me and say, "I am not much of a religious guy, but my respect for your family just went up four times!" This whole event proved to be a significant spiritual milestone in our son's life.

The point here is not to tell you what you can and cannot do on Sunday, but rather to remind you that your family schedule is a powerful influence in shaping your kids' hearts and values. The Scriptures have a lot to say about how we spend our time; in particular, how we spend our time on the Sabbath. If you are ready to slow down your life, consider a fresh approach to Sunday as a place to begin.

SIGNS OF A GOD-FILLED DAILY LIFE

What might a God-filled daily life look like? Here are a few practical ideas.

Talk about daily life from a spiritual perspective. God cares about every part of our day: our work, our relationships, our challenges. Do we use words with our kids that communicate God's presence with us throughout the day?

> "God really blessed me at work today. The problem I was having with my boss really took a turn for the better."

> "I am sorry that your friend made fun of you like that. That would really hurt my feelings. Why do you think God allowed that to happen?"

> "It doesn't make me happy to have to give you this punishment. But I am responsible before God to teach and train you to do what is right. So if I did not discipline you, I would be being disobedient to God."

Encourage family members to pray for each other.

"Kids, would you please pray for me today? I am really anxious about this meeting I have at work. I need your prayers."

"I know you have that big test tomorrow. Can we pray together for God to help you do your best?"

Let your kids see you spending time in prayer and Bible study. It is important for our kids to see us reading the Bible. Amy faithfully begins her day with the Lord in prayer and in the Scriptures. I love it when the kids wake up and find her spending time with God. It is an experience that they will never forget. Ask yourself, "Do my kids see that talking with God in prayer and seeking truth in His Word is a regular part of my life at home?"

Pray spontaneously. When you are in the car, and you see an accident on the side of the road, consider praying out loud, "God please bless them. Keep them safe. Heal them of any injuries they might have." Ask the kids to pray with you.

When you see a person who is in need, such as a person who is homeless, in addition to doing what you can to help that person, invite your kids to pray with you. "Lord, bless that man today. Give him an extra portion of your love."

Weave spontaneous thank-you prayers into the fabric of your day. When you receive a phone call from a family member who has just returned safely from a trip, pray out loud: "God, thank you for getting them home safely." When you see your son or daughter resist peer pressure and make a good choice, thank God for that: "Lord, thank you for giving him/her the strength and wisdom to do the right thing." Praying out loud is one of the best ways to create a God-filled, daily life.

Pray quickly for injuries. As soon as someone gets hurt or you find out someone is sick, pray out loud for him or her. The Christian response to sickness is: "pray first, see the doctor second." God has given us wisdom, medicine, and doctors, but God is the Great Physician. I can remember a few times as a child when I got seriously hurt. My mom would immediately pray for God to help me and heal me, and then we would jump in the car to head off to the emergency room. Too often, we make prayer our *last* resort after all human interventions have failed. Not only was I positively affected by my mother's prayers for my sicknesses and injuries, I was also positively affected when we saw some miraculous answers to those prayers. I will share one of those stories with you in a later chapter.

Talk about movies and music from a spiritual perspective. While I believe that kids today have way too much "screen time" in their lives, appropriate media can be used to spark significant spiritual conversations.

"What did you like about that movie? What didn't you like?"

"What were some of the messages in the movie?"

"How do those messages compare to God's truth?"

When our kids were younger, I took one occasion to be more intentional with a video we were about to watch. It was an old Star Wars cartoon. Before I turned it on, I told them that after the video we were going to play a quiz game, so I wanted them to watch very carefully. After the show, the quiz began. "Okay, kids, here is a true-or-false statement. Trees have spirits inside them just like people do." "Dad, that's silly. False!" "Okay, here is another one. Sometimes doing the right thing means people won't like you." "Yeah dad, that's true. We saw that in the video." After a few more questions and a little discussion, we enjoyed some ice cream. With little kids this type of interaction can be a game; with teens it can be a great way to get into some deep conversations.

Bring daily decisions back to the Bible. Your kids face decisions every day, some more difficult than others. They will come to you with all sorts of questions and dilemmas. Train yourself and your kids to respond to these questions with another question: "What has God said about this in His Word?" Remember our son's decision not to play baseball on the Sabbath? That was a complicated issue for us. We did not want to rely on our own intuition and human reasoning. First and foremost, we wanted to see what God said about how His people should approach the Sabbath. That is why we read the Scriptures with our son as part of the decision-making process.

Are you dealing with issues of dating? What does God say about this in the Bible? Are you facing issues about how to spend money? What does God say about this in the Bible? At this point, you probably think you could use some resources to help you use the Bible as a guide for everyday decisions. In a later chapter I will list some great resources that can help you apply the Bible to your family's daily decisions.

QUESTIONS FOR REFLECTION:

1. What are the core spiritual values that you want to see grow and develop in the heart of your child?

2. What are specific steps that you can take to create or modify your family schedule to cultivate these values?

3. Read Exodus chapter 20 and Isaiah chapter 58. Pay specific attention to the passages that focus on the Sabbath. How can you increasingly prioritize the Sabbath in your family schedule?

ENDNOTES

[1]Exodus 20:12, Deuteronomy 5:16, Matthew 15:4, Matthew 19:19, Mark 7:10, Mark 10:19, Luke 18:20, and Ephesians 6:2

[2]I understand that some faith traditions place the Sabbath on a different day of the week. I am choosing to talk about Sunday because since the resurrection of Christ this is the traditional day that Christians have set aside for worship, rest, family, and community.

CHAPTER 5

Getting to
the Heart

A Vision for a Safe Home

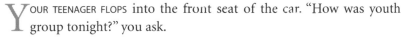

Y OUR TEENAGER FLOPS into the front seat of the car. "How was youth group tonight?" you ask.

"Fine."

"What did you learn?"

"Stuff."

There is an awkward silence the rest of the way home. This "conversation" repeats itself, in one form or another, week after week. What is going on? Why do teens seem to bristle when Mom or Dad gently ask personal questions, especially about spiritual things? I am convinced that moments like these are times of intense spiritual attack. Your son or daughter is being powerfully tempted with the message, "Don't open up to your parents. Don't give your heart to your mom or dad. It's okay to open up with friends or teachers or youth pastors . . . but don't be completely honest with your parents."

At the same time, there is an evil attack taking place against parents as we seek to connect at a heart level with our sons and daughters. We are under intense pressure to believe the myth of adolescence. The wisdom of the world, "confirmed" by psychology books, tries to tell us that it is normal, natural, and good for our children to go through an extended period of time called *adolescence.* The theory goes something like this: from the age of twelve to twenty-five your kids are going to be aloof, irresponsible, selfish, immature, and disrespectful persons. They will likely reject you, reject your faith, reject your church, experiment with sex, drugs, and alcohol, and if you can just endure these turbulent years it may be possible to have normal healthy relationship with them as adults. So when parents ask their teenagers about their spiritual lives and get one-word answers, the devil swoops in with the lie! "Oh yeah, these are the adolescent years. These are the years when your son isn't going to want to talk with you. His friends are more important now. His teachers and community leaders have more influence over him than you do, and this is a good thing. This is the way things ought to be. You just need to accept it and do your part." If Satan can get a teenager to pull his heart away from his parents and, at the same time, deceive his parents into accepting that a distant relationship with their teen son is normal and appropriate, the seeds are planted for broken relationships. God's plan for the teen years is very different from Satan's lies and the picture the world gives us.

The truth is that the teen years are vital years for parents and kids to be close! These are the years when your kids are making decisions that can affect the rest of their lives. The teen years are when young people need their parents more than ever, and when parents need to be close to their sons and daughters—more than ever. This deep, heart connection between a parent and a teenager does not just happen. You have to have a vision for it and actively work to achieve it.

WHAT IS A SAFE HOME?

When you think of the importance of having a safe home, what are the first things that come to mind? For many of us, our minds start racing with thoughts of outlet covers for the little ones, cabinet locks (which adults cannot seem to open either), smoke detectors, and so forth. Unfortunately, no matter how much we try to keep our kids from getting hurt, physical injuries are inevitable. In this chapter we are going to address the importance of building a home that is not only physically safe, but emotionally and spiritually safe as well.

We have already laid the foundation that our calling and primary responsibility as parents is to impress the hearts of our children with a love for God. This is our most important mission in life. It is a mission of the heart, and the heart of your child will only communicate with you and relate with you if he or she feels safe with you—physically, emotionally, and spiritually.

GOD SETS THE EXAMPLE

One of the best ways to learn how to be a godly parent is to consider how God parents us. In the Bible, He repeatedly emphasizes His desire to provide His children with peace, protection, and security. Paul prays for the Thessalonians with this in mind.

May the Lord of peace Himself give you peace at all times and in every way.

2 THESSALONIANS 3:16A

Our Heavenly Father tells us that He wants to drive fear out of our lives.

God did not give us a spirit of timidity, but a spirit of power, of love and of self-discipline.

2 TIMOTHY 1:7

There is no fear in love. But perfect love drives out fear, because fear has to do with punishment. The one who fears is not made perfect in love.

1 JOHN 4:18

This is not to say that God promises the Christian life will be free of pain and suffering. We live in a fallen world, and we can be assured that there will be both pain and persecution. Fear, however, is not in God's plan for His sons and daughters.

PERFECT LOVE DRIVES OUT FEAR

We all know what it is like to feel afraid. Where does fear come from? In what circumstances do we experience fear? There are two common causes of fear: being lost and feeling threatened. Can you remember getting lost when you were a child and the feelings that welled up inside of you? As adults, it is rare for us to be lost, but we still experience the feelings that come with threats. We lose employment, and fear is often not far behind. We come out of a store at night and on our way to our car we see a group of people watching our every move. Fear is present; we are on edge and our guard goes up. This same reaction takes place when fear is present in our relationships. If we do not feel safe with someone, our defense is up, our trust is low, and we are careful to guard our hearts.

Understanding these connections is vital to visionary parenting. If our kids feel lost or threatened, they will be afraid. Their defenses will rise, trust will decline, and worst of all, they will guard their hearts from us. If we want to have the opportunity to impress the hearts of our children with a love for God, we must do all we can to keep them from feeling lost and threatened in our homes.

How do we ensure that our kids do not feel lost? We do this by leading them. When a person is being led by a competent and experienced guide, there is no fear of getting lost. Imagine that you have chosen to scale Mount Everest. You have shelled out your $60,000 to your guides and Sherpas. After a few days, you finally arrive at 26,000 feet and are preparing to enter "the death zone." (If one is going to die on Everest, it is most likely to happen between 26,000 feet and the summit.) Up until this point, you have been climbing well and feeling good. In fact, you have been doing so well that your guides inform you that because of your excellent physical conditioning and clear mountaineering skills, they are going to head back down to base camp and let you finish the climb on your own. How would you react? I would be furious! I did not pay $60,000 to get from sea level to 26,000 feet! I paid to be guided through "the death zone."

If we fail to guide and direct our kids through the challenges of the teen years, we are no different than the guides who decide to leave the hiker alone for the hardest part of the climb. If we are disengaged from our children or are overly-permissive with them, they will end up feeling unsafe, cheated, abandoned, and angry. Is it true that overly-controlling parents cause anger in the hearts of their children? Yes, but in our culture today it is hard to find an overly-controlling parent. The plague of our day is overly-permissive parenting, and it is creating deep anger and resentment in this generation of children. Overly-permissive parenting sends a clear message to children: "I don't care enough about you to get involved in the details of your life." When a child or teen does not receive close, caring leadership from a parent, he will respond with insecurity and fear and will close off his heart.

YOUR HOME—A REFUGE

Life is hard. We all experience hurt and rejection. We all need a place to hide. In Psalm 32:7, our Heavenly Father reminds us that we can always hide in Him.

> *You are my hiding place; you will protect me from trouble and surround me with songs of deliverance.*

If God is a hiding place for His children, then we, as parents, should be a hiding place for our children. Where do your kids run when they are hurting? Where do they hide? Do they run home, straight to you, or do they run away as fast and far as they can? Many of us can remember as kids when we felt that the last place we wanted to be was home because of the pain and lack of safety there. Amy and I pray that God will make our home, and our hearts, the perfect hiding place for our children. This is not just a vision for parents with small children but for parents with adult children as well. If my son is having a crisis in his marriage some day, I want his first instinct to be to pick up the phone to call his dad. If my daughter, as an adult one day, has the desire to be mentored by an older woman, I want her first phone call to be to her mom. This is not to say that I do not want my adult children to benefit from the counsel and support of other people. I simply want them to know that the mission of my parenting does not end when they leave my home. Does parenting change when our children become adults? Of course it does. But we must reject the modern philosophy of parenting that teaches "when they leave, we are done."

CREATING A SAFE HOME

Because our parenting mission is focused on the hearts of our children, we must do all we can to create safe relationships and to establish a safe home. Here are four principles to help get us started.

1: Unconditional Acceptance Creates Security

When my son RW was around three years old, I would ask him, "Why does daddy love you?" I never told him what to say, but he always gave me one of two answers. He would either say, "Because you love me!" or "Because I'm your boy!" For the second answer, he puffed out his chest as far as possible. I used to laugh at his cute little answers. However, the more I thought about it, the more I realized that not only were his answers correct, but they were the *only* two correct answers. Why do I love my son? Because I love him and he is my boy. He cannot do anything to change that sort of love! It has nothing to do with what he looks like, what he accomplishes, or even how he behaves. Do I truly love my son this perfectly? Of course I do not. I wish I did. But I know a Heavenly Father who does love His children this way.

Have you ever wondered why God loves you? There are two answers. He loves you because He loves you and you are His child. It has nothing to do with what you look like, what you accomplish, or how you behave. Some of you grew up in church hearing, "God loves you." You may have heard it so much that you became numb to it. If we are going to truly love our children, we must first respond to the love of God. God knows all the sick things that you have ever thought, and He loves you. He knows all the evil you have ever done, yet He loves you. His love for you is not based on you! It is based on His choice to love you, and the fact that He chose to create you. When this truth finally sinks into the deep places of our hearts, we are flooded with an incomparable sense of peace, rest, and safety. We stop running and find our rest in Him.

It is God's desire for our children to experience this same unconditional love from us, so that their hearts will be prepared to experience unconditional love from Him. We can begin by committing to give our children more than performance-based affirmation. How often do we tell our children that we are proud of them apart from anything they have done? How frequently do we tell our kids we love them "just because"? One of the questions that I routinely asked high school students in counseling sessions was, "Do you feel like your parents love you more when you do right and love you less when you mess up?" The majority said yes. In short, they felt their parents loved them *conditionally.*

My father had many character problems, but one thing he did for me was to verbally express his love for me. My dad frequently said to me, "Bobby, if you robbed a bank, I would still love you." You may find that somewhat silly or insignificant. What my dad was trying to tell me, in his own way, was that he was not going to stop loving me even if I did something terrible. It made my feel safe and secure in my dad's love. There are powerful words and phrases that our children need to hear:

"I love you no matter what."

"I am proud of you just because you are you."

"I will always love you no matter what you do."

"There is nothing you can do to make me love you any less, and there is nothing you can do that will make me love you any more."

The purpose here is not to build what the world would call self-esteem in our children. Rather, we are to do all we can to parent our children with full grace and full truth. I recently had a mother of two preschoolers ask me, "How can I discipline my kids in a way that will never make them feel like they are a bad person?" She was more than a little shocked when I explained to her that our goal is not to ensure that our kids never feel bad about themselves. In fact, if our children never come to the realization that they are inherently sinful, they will never repent, believe in Christ, and be saved! They must understand that we all commit sin because of our inherent sin nature. The last thing in the world we want to do is shield our children from this fact. The sooner they realize they are sinners in need of a savior, the sooner they will receive the love, grace, and forgiveness of God.

2: Defending Your Child Creates Security

Imagine that it is recess time at the elementary school. A couple of kids get into a fight. It usually does not take too long for someone to throw down the gauntlet and say, "I am going to get my dad." To which the other boy says, "Oh yeah? Well my dad could kick the tar out of your dad!" The reason this scene gets replayed on school yards across the country is because kids have a core instinct that when they get in trouble someone will protect them! Their hearts want to believe, "Mom and Dad will stick up for me! I am not alone. I have protectors." Ultimately, our hearts were built to find safety and protection in Father God.

You are my hiding place; you will protect me from trouble and surround me with songs of deliverance.

PSALM 32:7

"Because of the oppression of the weak, and the groaning of the needy, I will now arise", says the LORD. "I will protect them from those who malign them."

PSALM 12:5

This is a theme that runs from Genesis to Revelation. God has compassion for the oppressed, and He uses His power on their behalf. If our children are under attack out there in the world, they must *know* that their parents are right beside them, prepared to arise and defend them.

Let us suppose that your seventh-grade son is being bullied. Incidents have gone from weekly to daily. You sit down with your son to come up with a strategy to deal with this problem. Strategy number one: ignore the bully. The next day your son executes the strategy flawlessly. Sadly, he still ends up crammed into a locker. We need a new plan. So you come up with strategy number two: stand up to the bully. The next day, your son does exactly that. He stands toe-to-toe with the bully and tells him that he is not going to take this any more. As a reward, he gets a black eye and is put back in the locker. Hmm. Now we need another plan. Strategy number three: ignore the bully. Your son stares at you in disbelief as you offer this suggestion. "Dad, didn't we try that already? It didn't seem to work very well." You reply, "I know son, but maybe it will work this time. You never know." Your son puts his head down and walks slowly out of the room.

In this situation, the dad gave his son decent advice. But when these first steps failed to stop the bullying, the dad was not willing to take it to the next level. When our kids are under attack physically, emotionally, or spiritually a time comes when a father or mother says, "Enough is enough! I am going take care of this for you, son. I am going to meet with the principal today, and I will meet with this bully's parents tomorrow. You have done what I have asked you to do, and now it is time for you to sit back and let me fight this battle for you."

Where are the moms and dads who are willing to do what it takes to protect their kids when they need protecting? Too many parents seem to express, "Oh, but I don't want to make trouble. I don't want to get anyone upset." Is this what our Heavenly Father does in response to the persecution of His children? No! God comes to the point when He says, "Enough is enough; the battle is now mine! Be still and you will see the power of God."

There is a powerful scene in the movie *The Two Towers,* the second film in the Lord of the Rings trilogy. The armies of evil are marching into the land of Rohan, bent on conquest. Aragorn pleads with King

Theodin, ruler of Rohan, to muster his horsemen and ride out to meet them! Theodin answers, "I will not risk open war." To which Aragorn replies, "Open war is upon you, whether you would risk it or not." There are times when our children need defending. There are times when the battle against our children has already begun, and the question is whether or not we are going to fight.

The point here is not that we need to become Rambo parents, but that we embrace our biblical role and responsibility to protect our children. Do you know what happens to kids who keep getting bullied, whose parents will not do what it takes to protect them? They stop talking about it. They slowly stop sharing their fears and problems with Mom and Dad. Their hearts learn that the way to make it through this life is to take care of themselves. They say, "My parents love me, but not enough to help me." In time, that same sentiment is projected on their view of God. "God loves me, but not enough to help me. He is very busy. He doesn't have time for my problems."

Being the protector of our children does not mean we shield them from the painful consequences of their choices. If they get arrested for selling drugs, it does not mean we bail them out of jail as soon as they call. God does not protect us from the painful consequences of our sin. He loves us and knows that if He does not allow us to reap what we sow, we will not grow. Do not confuse protecting your children with shielding them from the pain of consequences.

Tragically, some parents not only fail to protect their children, they directly abuse them. God created parents to be just like Him—loving, safe protectors. When parents are the opposite of that and abuse their children, it is a great evil. Sadly, abuse sometimes creates a dual wound in the heart of a child. The first is the wound and hurt that comes from the abusive parent; the second is the wound of not being protected by the other parent. If your spouse is hurting your children, do not delay in getting help. God created you to be a protector of your children. This is a battle they cannot fight on their own. Call your pastor. Call an abuse hotline. If you know of a child in your extended family, your church, or your neighborhood who is being abused or who is in danger, do whatever you can to inform the appropriate authorities.

3: Stating and Living God's Order Creates Security

One of the best ways to create a safe home is to do all in our power to build our family with biblical priorities. The more our homes reflect God's structure for the family, the more the hearts of our children will be at peace. So what is God's structure for the family?

Moms, let's think of your role in the home first. As a mother, who is to be your first love? As we learned in the Great Commandment, your most important role is to love God with all your heart. Your personal relationship with Him is to be your highest priority. Who does God call you to love next? For those of you who are married, it is your husband. Your love for him is to be your second priority. Your children fill the third place in God's order for your life. Dads, our first priority is to love and obey God. Our second priority, if married, is to love our wives as Christ loved the church and laid down His life for her. Our third priority is to love, pastor, and disciple our children.

The divine order is God, spouse, and then kids. It is not complicated. But living life in this order can be a great challenge. I believe that we need to talk about this order frequently with our children. Multiple times a month I tell my kids, "I want you to know that I love Jesus, I love your mom, and I love you." Sometimes I will ask them, "What are the three things Daddy loves best?" Hopefully they know the answer: "God, mom, and us!"

One night I was putting the kids to bed and had just repeated "the love list" to them again. Lissy, then five years old, said, "Daddy, why am I last? Why am I number three?" She wasn't overly pleased with her ranking in this system! I did my best to answer the question. "Lissy, if I didn't love your mom, do you think I would be able to love you my very best?" She said, "No." "If I didn't love Jesus, do you think that I would be able to love mom my very best?" Even at five years old, she got it.

As you know, I spent the last of my growing up years being raised by a single mom. Many of you are single dads or moms. Do not be discouraged! God has a clear order for you as well. Love Him, and love your kids. Talk about the ordering of your life with them often. "Son, I want you to know that I love Jesus and that I love you." Consider the words of God from Psalm 68:4–6:

Sing to God, sing praise to his name, extol him who rides on the clouds—his name is the LORD—and rejoice before him. A father to the fatherless, a defender of widows, is God in his holy dwelling.

After my parents divorced, God proved Himself to my mother, to my brother, and to me. The divorce was beyond painful, but God never left us. If you are single, I encourage you to trust in the promises of God. First, give your heart to God and seek to obey His Word at every point. Second, give your heart to your children, and embrace your primary calling in this world to help them get safely home to their Father in Heaven.

Talking about God's order for the home is important, but if our kids do not see these priorities in action, our own words will work against us. Our kids feel insecure when they see us say one thing and do another. I have a lot of growing to do in this area. I so much want my children to see my love for God and my love for Amy. Unfortunately, they see a lot of my love for me. Do your kids ever "catch you" in prayer or in Scripture study? I struggle to get up early in the morning to pray and ready my Bible. But I am working hard to develop this habit so that when the kids get up the first thing they will see is Dad spending time with the Lord.

4: Parental Blessing Creates Security and Peace in the Hearts of Our Children

We have already discovered that a great way to learn about parenting is to follow God's methods of parenting us. One of the things that our Heavenly Father does throughout Scripture is to give blessings to His children. Right after God created Adam and Eve, He blessed them saying, "Be fruitful and increase in number; fill the earth and subdue it" (Genesis 1:28b). It is the first of numerous blessings that God directly expressed to His children. Theological dictionaries frequently define a blessing as, "the bestowal of good." When God blesses us He is saying, "I wish this for you. I give this to you. I desire this for you." Not only does God speak blessings to His children, He encourages parents to do the same for their children.

Many parents in the Bible understood the power of blessing their children. When Jacob was reunited with his lost son Joseph, who had become the prince of Egypt, Jacob asked Joseph if he could bless his grandchildren.

"Bring [your sons] to me, so I may bless them." . . . *Then he blessed Joseph and said, "May the God before whom my fathers Abraham and Isaac walked, the God who has been my shepherd all my life to this day, the angel who has delivered me from all harm—may he bless these boys. May they be called by my name and the names of my fathers Abraham and Isaac, and may they increase greatly upon the earth."*

GENESIS 48:9, 15–16

Wow! What I would not give to have had a grandfather speak words like that over me. God has given the power of blessing to parents and grandparents. Taking the time to bless our children with words of prayer and affirmation can transform their lives. Blessings are not magic formulas. They are a powerful spiritual tool that God has given to parents and grandparents to nurture faith and character in the hearts of their kids. When parents regularly speak blessings to their children, it increases their sense of peace and safety.

My mother blessed me every day when I left for school. She would meet me at the side door, put her arm around me, and speak the words of blessing from Numbers 6:24–26.

The LORD bless you and keep you; the LORD make his face shine upon you and be gracious to you; the LORD turn his face toward you and give you peace.

I can remember it as if it were yesterday. It was powerful! It was regular. It is now my great honor to bless my children with the same blessing each night before they go to bed. My mother used these words to bless me, and now her grandchildren hear them too. As my kids lay in bed, I go to each one of them individually. "May the Lord bless you and keep you. May the Lord make His face to shine upon you, and give you peace, all the days of your life." It is one of the best parts of my day . . . and theirs. In fact, they will not let me forget to do it! They will remind me, "Daddy! You forgot to bless us!"

One night I sat on the bed next to Lissy and spoke these words of blessing to her. As I talked, she grimaced and almost writhed with discomfort. I said, "Lissy, I thought you liked it when I blessed you." She replied, "I like to hear it, not smell it." Apparently, my oral hygiene was not up to par that evening. If you are going to begin this practice of blessing your kids, brush your teeth!

HOW SAFE DO YOUR KIDS FEEL?

One of the best ways to find out how safe your kids feel with you is to try and have a direct conversation with them about it. If your kids are older than five years old, consider asking them some of these questions:

> *"On a scale of 1–10, how accepted do you feel by me (your mom/ dad)?"*

> *"On a scale of 1–10, how much peace do you feel in our home?"*

> *"On a scale of 1–10, how comfortable do you feel talking with me about your feelings?"*

Let us imagine that you ask this last question and your daughter says, "Well, I guess I would have to say . . . three." You quickly explode with, "THREE! How could you say three! Haven't I always told you that you can tell me anything? I can't believe that you would even consider saying three!" If you respond like this, is it any wonder your daughter said three? If you want to have open-hearted conversations with your kids, be prepared to hear things you may not want to hear. When your sons or daughters open up to you, affirm them . Thank them for telling you the truth . . . even if the truth is not very pleasant. Remember that the purpose of creating a safe home is so that your sons or daughters will never hesitate to let you into their hearts.

LOVE ME

"Love Me" is the title of one of my favorite songs, performed by J. J. Heller. I believe the questions asked in this song are asked by every child and teenager.

> *He cries in the corner where nobody sees*
> *He's the kid with the story no one would believe*
> *He prays every night, "Dear God won't you please*
> *Could you send someone here who will love me?"*

> *Who will love me for me?*
> *Not for what I have done or what I will become*
> *Who will love me for me?*
> *'Cause nobody has shown me what love*
> *What love really means*

Her office is shrinking a little each day
She's the woman whose husband has run away
She'll go to the gym after working today
Maybe if she was thinner
Then he would've stayed
And she says . . .

Who will love me for me?
Not for what I have done or what I will become
Who will love me for me?
'Cause nobody has shown me what love, what love really means

He's waiting to die as he sits all alone
He's a man in a cell who regrets what he's done
He utters a cry from the depths of his soul
"Oh Lord, forgive me, I want to go home"

Then he heard a voice somewhere deep inside
And it said
"I know you've murdered and I know you've lied
I have watched you suffer all of your life
And now that you'll listen, I'll tell you that I . . ."

I will love you for you
Not for what you have done or what you will become
I will love you for you
I will give you the love
The love that you never knew [1]

In the heart of every child is this question: "Who will love me for me?" Let us answer these cries of our sons and daughters! Dad will love you for you. Mom will love you for you. You are safe here.

QUESTIONS FOR REFLECTION:

1. Study Psalm 119:165 and Isaiah 32:17. What is the pre-requisite for having peace in our homes?

2. Go to the beginning and end of each New Testament letter. See if you can find examples of blessings. Write these down on a 3x5 card. Begin to use them to bless your children.

3. Would your children say that your love for them rises and falls with their performance? What active steps could you take to communicate unconditional acceptance to them?

4. Do you have any areas of concern regarding the physical, emotional, or spiritual safety of your children? Share those with your spouse, a close Christian friend, or if needed a pastor or Christian counselor.

ENDNOTE

[1]J. J. and Dave Heller. *Only Love Remains*, "Love Me," Produced by Mitch Dane. Released by Stone Table Records, 2006

CHAPTER 6

A Father's Mission

A Vision for Biblical Fatherhood

W E NOW TURN OUR FOCUS to two unique callings from God: fatherhood and motherhood. Dads, be sure to read both this chapter and the next chapter on motherhood. Moms, I urge you not to skip this chapter on biblical fatherhood. As the father in my home, it is vital that I understand the role God wants me to play, but I also need to understand God's role for Amy as the mother so I can encourage her. In the same way, if Amy does not know what God calls me to be as a father, how can she help me be successful?

We are only one paragraph into this chapter, and I can already feel the tension. To utter the phrase "gender roles in the home" or even worse "biblical roles for men and women" is like tossing a grenade into a conversation. Our culture fights against any differentiation between men and women and, as a result, many Christians have chosen to be silent about this subject for fear of conflict or rejection. I believe that our silence as to what God says about the role of the father and the mother in the home has led to great confusion, pain, and suffering in our families.

EQUAL AND DIFFERENT

God created men and women with equal value, worth, and dignity. This is taught throughout the Scriptures.

> *So God created man in his own image, in the image of God he created him; male and female he created them.*

GENESIS 1:27

In the beginning of this verse, when it says "God created man," the word *man* means mankind or humankind. The passage goes on to say that God made two kinds of "man"—the male "man" and the female "man." Both men and women are made in the image of God and stand on equal footing before Him. In Galatians 3:28, Paul reiterates that men and women are of equal value.

> *There is neither Jew nor Greek, slave nor free, male nor female, for you are all one in Christ Jesus.*

So far so good, but here is where feathers start getting ruffled. While the Bible teaches that men and women have equal value and importance, it also teaches that God created us differently because He has different purposes that He calls us to fulfill. Men and women are wired differently by our Creator and are called to fulfill different roles as parents. Obviously, God did not create men to give birth to children. That is a role reserved for women. God did create men with special responsibility to protect and defend children after birth.

I have had many people in my office who resist the idea that there are particular roles for men and women in the family. Consider this situation. You are sleeping soundly in bed with your spouse. You jolt awake to the sound of crashing glass and someone moving through the house . . . toward the baby's bedroom. Who gets up out of bed, grabs the bat, and goes out to stop the bad guy? Is it the woman or the man? When I present this scenario to couples in my office, the wife quickly points at her husband! If you would agree that, generally speaking, it is the man's role to protect the family in face of danger, then you believe that there are role distinctions for men and women. The question then, is not whether or not there are different roles but *what* are the different roles God calls us to fulfill. Thankfully, because of the Bible we are not left in the dark to figure these things out for ourselves. Let us look at specific Scriptures to see what God has to say about the calling of fatherhood.

THE IMPORTANCE OF FATHERHOOD

In the past decade much research has demonstrated the important role that a father plays in the lives of his children.[1] I am so glad that this research was done! Now it is proven beyond a shadow of a doubt: dads matter. I find it comical that some seemed to have needed a research study to come to this conclusion.

Did you ever play with dominoes when you were a kid? You carefully set them up in a line, spaced them evenly, gave the first one a little tap, and down they went. The Bible lays out a series of principles that have a similar domino effect. Consider the following connections:

As the man goes, so goes the marriage.

As the marriage goes, so goes the family.

As the family goes, so goes the local church.

As the local church goes, so goes the nation and the Great Commission.

My beliefs, actions, and words set the tone for my relationship with Amy and our entire family. She responds to my leadership. If I set the right tone and lead well, the likelihood of warmth, love, health, and blessing overflowing to my family is very high. I know from vast personal experience that the opposite is also true.

THE ROLE OF A FATHER TO LOVE HIS WIFE

We cannot talk about a vision for biblical fatherhood without first talking about biblical principles for husbands. (Although some of you dads may be single, let me urge you not to skip over this part of the book. God may call you to marriage in the future, and if you have sons, now is the time to start training them to be godly husbands and fathers.)

A primary section of Scripture regarding the role of the husband is found in Ephesians 5:25–26.

Husbands, love your wives, just as Christ loved the church and gave himself up for her to make her holy, cleansing her by the washing with water through the word.

This is a power-packed sentence in which we find three core callings from God. Men, what is the first thing God calls us to do with our wives? *Love them.* "Husbands, love your wives." Many in our culture accuse Christians of believing that men are to dominate their wives and that their wives are to be doormats. This is madness! Not only have I never personally heard a Christian preacher or writer utter such a thing, but here in black and white, we have a command from God for husbands to *love* their wives!

We need to dig deeper into what this means. God gives us a definition of love that is very different from the world's understanding. Love is defined by God for us in 1 Corinthians 13:4–7.

> *Love is patient, love is kind. It does not envy, it does not boast, it is not proud. It is not rude, it is not self-seeking, it is not easily angered, it keeps no record of wrongs. Love does not delight in evil but rejoices with the truth. It always protects, always trusts, always hopes, always perseveres.*

So if I say I love Amy, I am not saying I have warm feelings toward her. In my desk drawer I have a little card with these words on it:

> *When it comes to Amy, I am patient. When it comes to Amy, I am kind. When it comes to Amy, I don't envy. I don't boast around her. I don't think I am better than she is. I am not rude to her. I don't look out for what I want, and I don't get angry easily. I don't keep track of the wrong things she has done. I am not happy when bad things happen to her, and I rejoice when good things happen to her and she grows closer to God. I always protect her. I always trust her. I always think the best of her, and I never tire of doing any of these things.*

While these words may be written on a card in my desk drawer, is this an accurate description of how I love Amy? Not even close. I fail to live up to the things on this list every day. But I keep the list in front of me for two reasons. First, if I say I love my wife, I have to be clear about what I am saying. This is the measure of how I want to treat my wife. Second, choosing to use God's definition of love rather than the world's definition keeps me in an attitude of humility and prayer before God. I do not have what it takes to love Amy like this. I do not have the character, the strength, or the discipline. The only way it is going to happen, is if God supernaturally works in and through me, and that is what I continually ask Him to do. Men, we need to be very clear that loving our wives is a supernatural calling and responsibility. Our only hope of success is humbling ourselves before God and asking Him to make us the husbands He created us to be.

LAY YOUR LIFE DOWN

The first instruction for the husband in Ephesians 5 is to love his wife as Christ loved the church. The second command is to serve his wife.

> *Husbands love your wives, just as Christ loved the church, and gave himself up for her.*

EPHESIANS 5:25

Godly men give up their lives for their wives, just as Christ gave up His life for the church. Remember the story about the intruder walking through the house? No man I know is going to give the bat to his wife and jump under the bed! One of the ways men show love is by serving their wives, even in the threat of danger.

I am confident that if such a situation were to arise in your house, you would bravely protect your family. You would lay down your life for your wife. But will you lay down your hobbies this weekend to prioritize your time with her and get the needed projects done around the house? Will you lay down your Blackberry or the TV remote for the evening to give her your undivided attention? When forced with a choice to disappoint a friend or your wife, which one do you choose? Personally, I find the every-day challenge to "lay down my life" for Amy more difficult than the crisis situations.

TO MAKE HER HOLY

The first command to husbands is to love. The second command is to serve. Now we come to the point of it all, the central mission of a husband.

> *Husbands, love your wives, just as Christ loved the church and gave himself up for her, to make her holy, cleansing her by the washing with water through the word.*

EPHESIANS 5:25–27

Why does God want me to love Amy? Why does He want me to serve her? The purpose is to make her holy. Men, have you ever wondered why God chose to bring your wife into your life? Here is your answer. God gave you your wife so you would do all in your power to encourage faith in her heart and to help her become the woman that God created her to be. When we put these three commands together we get LOVE—SERVE—LEAD.

Do not miss the order! God's word is precise, and we need to pay attention to it. Men, what happens if you try to lead a woman without first loving her and serving her? The very thought of it sends shivers up the spine. If a man tries to lead a woman without the foundation of love and service, her heart will quickly fill with bitterness and resentment. God did not create women to be led by men who do not love them.

Men, if you seek to commit yourself to love your wife, to serve her, and to become the spiritual leader in your marriage, you should prepare yourself for major spiritual attack. Satan will throw everything at you to prevent you from being the man God calls you to be, and his attack on you will be strategic. Satan does not want you to love your wife, and He will try and prevent it. If you have a warm and caring relationship, that is not necessarily a threat to him and his designs on your family and your children. But he does not want you to lay down your life for your wife, and he will continually tempt you to serve your own needs rather than hers. However, a man who serves his wife still is not a grave threat to Satan. However, if you want to obey the third command, if you desire to make it the primary mission of your life to encourage faith and character in your wife and children, that Satan will not tolerate, and he will do all in his power to prevent it.

Let me illustrate how this spiritual attack happens. Men, consider the following three questions:

- Do you believe that praying with your wife is an important thing to do?

- Do you believe that God wants you to pray with your wife?

- Is praying with your wife easy or hard, compared to climbing Mount Everest? (In other words, is it easy or hard to hold your wife's hand, and say a few words to God?)

Most guys are going to answer yes, yes, and easy. Now for the fourth question:

- Do you struggle to pray faithfully and consistently with your wife?

Most of us reply with another yes. This makes no sense! We believe that praying with our wives is important. We believe God wants us to do it, and we know it is physically easy to do. Despite all that, men frequently struggle to pray faithfully their wives. How could this be? The reason this is played out in millions of Christian homes around the country is because we fail to identify another part of the equation. Although prayer with my wife is important, God wants me to do it, and it is easy to do, *Satan does all in his power to prevent me from doing it!* So Amy and I, like so many other Christian couples, struggle to pray as a couple.

For the first twelve years of our marriage, our prayer life as a couple was inconsistent at best. By God's grace we are finally breaking through and experiencing consistency in a short time of prayer together before we go to sleep. But the battle is not over! Amy and I have prayed together almost every night for the past year. Yet, I know what will happen when I get in bed tonight. The Holy Spirit will say to me, "Rob, you should pray with Amy now." I will then immediately feel a sense of discomfort and embarrassment, mixed with some laziness. Where do all those feelings come from? They certainly do not come from Amy. She loves it when I lead us in prayer. God would never lead me astray. Those are moments of spiritual attack from the enemy, who is desperate to do all he can to prevent Amy and me from coming before the Lord with one heart in prayer. Why is he so desperate to prevent my taking any role of spiritual leadership in our marriage? Because once that happens, our family begins to function with transformational spiritual power! Our marriage and our home become a threat to Satan and a dynamic ministry tool in the hands of God.

Is prayer an area of struggle for you in your marriage? A great place to begin praying together is at "collision" time. Collision time is the moment of the day when your world and your wife's world collide. It may be when you come home from work at the end of the day. It may be when your wife returns with the kids from sports practice. Whenever you and your wife are finally home after the day's activities, walk directly over to her, take her hand, and pray something like this: "God, thank you for bringing us home safely. Please bless our marriage and our family tonight. We pray this in Jesus' name, amen." This ten-second spiritual investment can dramatically affect your relationship. Many of our conflicts happen when our worlds collide. You bring the stress from your day; she brings the stress from her day, and boom! This brief moment of prayer begins your time together on a unified path. More importantly, God hears and answers prayers. This short prayer is not some magic formula or incantation that makes people happy. Rather, it is an appeal to God to use His power on your behalf to unify your hearts and your home. It is a prayer God loves to answer.

OUR MARRIAGE AND OUR KIDS

How a man relates to his wife dramatically affects the entire family, and directly affects the souls of his children. When a man loves, serves, and leads his wife, he creates security for his children. I have lost track of the number of parents who have brought their teen to me for counseling with the message, "Fix my kid!" After spending some time with the teen, it often becomes apparent that the struggles he or she is dealing with stem from the fact that the parents cannot stand each other! One of the greatest gifts you can give your children is a committed, growing, Christian marriage.

Our marriages not only have a direct affect on our children while they are growing up, but also set the stage for their future marriages. My father's life was a great illustration of this. My dad was born during the flu epidemic of 1918. His mother became ill toward the end of her pregnancy and died shortly after my dad was born. He was born prematurely, which was a life-threatening situation in those days. As a result, he spent the first year of his life in the hospital. His father already had two boys and, with the loss of his wife, did not feel that he could take care of another baby. So when my dad was one year old, he was adopted by his uncle and his aunt, who were brother and sister. It was not an incestuous relationship, rather a single man and single woman, brother and sister, sharing a home together. While his aunt and uncle provided for my dad and genuinely cared for him, he never saw a marriage work. He had so many strikes against him! Much of the rest of his life was spent looking for love, attachment, and connection. He was married four times, with my mother being his fourth wife. He suffered greatly without the blessing of a mother and father who loved each other.

This is not to say that if you are divorced or you are in a struggling marriage your children are doomed to be in a broken marriage themselves. God is in the business of taking broken things and making them whole. That is exactly what He did with my family.

THE ROLE OF A FATHER TO BE A SPIRITUAL LEADER

Most Christian men know that God calls them to be the spiritual leaders of their families, at the same time they are plagued with guilt that they do not measure up. Satan would love to have you wallow in that guilt and keep struggling. The journey to becoming spiritual leaders starts with the recognition that we do not have what it takes to do this. God has to work in us, empower us, and change us. How can we lead our families in a direction that we are not going ourselves? If your wife is more passionate about growing in her faith than you are about growing in your faith, your marriage is upside down. I challenge you to take one minute for the next thirty days and pray this prayer. "God, please turn my heart to my wife and to my children. Do what needs to be done in my heart and in my life so that I can lead my family in faith."

God gives us another step to becoming spiritual leaders in Ephesians 5:25–26:

> *Husbands, love your wives, just as Christ loved the church and gave himself up for her to make her holy, cleansing her by the washing with water through the word.*

Where do I start, if I want to encourage faith in the heart of my wife? I do everything I can to bring the Bible into the center of our relationship. God gives us a vision for marriage where husbands and wives take time to read the Bible together, talk about it, and allow it to transform them. In my experience, the attack from the enemy is even stronger in this area of my marriage than in the area of prayer. Part of my problem over the years was that my expectations were too high. I pictured an hour a day of studying through a couples' devotional. Some of you have bought one of these books (or your wife has bought one), and while these are wonderful tools, the book is probably on the shelf gathering dust. Most couples are not able to go from never reading the Bible together to doing a daily, in-depth study together. Amy loves to quote Chesterton who said, "If something is worth doing, it is worth doing poorly." We procrastinate or wait to do a lot of things because we are only willing to do them if we can do them right. When it comes to reading God's Word with our wives, we must be willing to do it poorly rather than not at all. Reading one chapter, once a month, is better than never reading at all. Grabbing a few minutes to sit on the couch and read a

Psalm is a few minutes well-spent, even if you have to squeeze it into a busy schedule. Once you start doing it "poorly," your heart connection will deepen with one another and with the Lord, and He will give you the grace to make your time with Him a higher priority.

THE ROLE OF THE FATHER TO INSTRUCT HIS CHILDREN IN THE LORD

While Ephesians 5 contains the keynote passage for Christian husbands, in Ephesians 6 we receive our marching orders for what it means to be a godly father.

Fathers, do not exasperate your children; instead, bring them up in the training and instruction of the Lord.

EPHESIANS 6:4

God knows how the male mind operates. We usually like to keep things short and sweet. So He gives us guidance about one thing we are not to do and two things we are to do. He says, "Do not exasperate your children." This word *exasperate* in the original Greek language means to rouse to deep anger. This is *not* saying that God never wants you to do anything that will upset your kids. You may handle a discipline situation perfectly, and calmly hand down an appropriate consequence, which results in a lot of anger from your child. We are talking about something much deeper. Fathers are not to provoke anger and bitterness in the souls of their children. Many of us know exactly what God is talking about here because we have had to deal with deep resentment toward our own fathers.

We can all agree that we do not want to anger our children! No father wants angry children. Thankfully, God gives us the counteraction. If we do not want to fuel anger in the hearts of our children, then we must obey the second part of the verse: "instead, bring them up in the training and instruction of the Lord." When a father fails to do these things, anger and resentment are not far behind. God built your child's heart to respond positively to your love and leadership!

Ephesians 6:4 echoes the Great Commandment from Deuteronomy 6:5–7.

Love the LORD your God with all your heart and with all your soul and with all your strength. These commandments that I give you today are to be upon your hearts. Impress them on your children. Talk about them when you sit at home and when you walk along the road, when you lie down and when you get up.

Our primary responsibility as fathers, according to the God who made our kids and gave them to us, is to bring them up in the training and instruction of the Lord. There are two key words in Ephesians 6:4: *training* and *instruction*. One is an action word and one is a communication word.

What does it mean to bring up our children in the training of the Lord? The original Greek word for *training* refers to the physical training athletes undertook before their games. If my son JD and I go out to the driveway to shoot some baskets, we are doing basketball *training*. We are not playing the game, but our training will help him get ready for the game. God calls us as fathers to do spiritual training, spiritual exercises, with our kids. We are to practice spiritual life with our children. We are to pray *with* our children. We are to read the Bible *with* our children. We are to worship in church *with* our children (more on that in a later chapter). We are to serve our neighbors *with* our children. Whenever we do spiritual activities with our children we are "bringing them up in the training of the Lord."

We are to lead with spiritual action, but we are also to lead with spiritual communication. *"Bring them up in the instruction of the Lord."* The Greek word for *instruction* means verbal instruction, correction, and encouragement. A lot of men gravitate to the lead-by-example approach to fathering. We tell ourselves, "My kids are going to learn what it means to be a Christian and a good person by watching me. After all, more is caught than taught." But if my kids determine what it means to be a godly man only by watching me, this is a very bad plan! I sin on a daily basis, frequently in front of my wife and children, and often against them. I ask my family's forgiveness for something pretty much every day. My example is just not good enough. This is not to say that living an exemplary life is not important, but in this passage, God calls us to make every effort to live right with our kids *and* to talk right with our kids. Our actions *and* our words are powerful!

THE POWER OF A FATHER'S WORDS

When you walk into a store and look at all the items on the shelves, you notice that some are expensive and some are cheap. Why? What determines how valuable things are? There are two fundamental economic principles that drive value: supply and demand. How much will you pay me for a bucket of dirt? You will probably pay nothing. Why? Because there is a huge supply of dirt and very low demand, which makes a bucket of dirt next to worthless. On the other hand, how much will you pay me for a bucket of diamonds? You probably could not afford it! Why? Because the supply of diamonds is very low and the demand is very high, which makes them extremely valuable and extremely expensive.

Consider with me the value of a father's words. In a typical home, is there a high supply or a low supply of a father's words of spiritual nurture, guidance, and encouragement for his wife and children? Typically, the supply is low. On the other side, what is the demand and desire for these words from his wife and children? The desire is extremely high. What does this mean? A father's words of spiritual nurture and instruction are powerful and priceless!

DO YOUR KIDS LOVE WHAT YOU LOVE?

All my kids are Red Sox fans. This did not happen by accident. I grew up in Connecticut and rooted for the Red Sox with my dad. I wanted my kids to be Red Sox fans too! They saw me excited as the Sox made the playoffs. They would watch the World Series games with me. (It sounds strange to talk about the Red Sox in the World Series, but it is a pleasant thing to be getting used to). I bought them all Sox shirts and hats. Laynie, even at two years old, loved wearing her David Ortiz shirt with Little Papi on the back of it. Why would I go through such trouble to get my kids to like the Red Sox? It is not primarily because I want them to be fans of that team or that sport, but because I want them to love what I love and enjoy what I enjoy. As fathers, we literally have the power to shape what our kids love! I intentionally did what I could to encourage my kids' love of the Sox, and I succeeded. God calls us to use the power and influence He has given us as dads to impress the hearts of our children with a love for Jesus.

I get concerned when I think about the issue of sports with my kids. More specifically, I am troubled about the issue of sports and me! Do my children see me get more excited when a game is coming up on TV or when we are getting ready to go to church? What message is sent if I excitedly jump out of my seat at a home run, but I look like I am just going through the motions when I sing praise to God during family worship or on Sunday mornings? What do your children see you get most passionate about? Those are the things they know are most important to you.

Earlier we talked about the potential for spiritual attack from Satan in our marriages. That potential is no less intense in our parenting. Satan does not want you to provide for your kids, but he can tolerate it. He does not want you to protect your kids; in fact, he would rather you abuse them. He does not want you to be involved in your kids' activities, but he can put up with it. What the enemy cannot tolerate is when you assume your God-given role to be the pastor and spiritual shepherd of your children. You can be sure he will mount a full-scale attack against you to prevent this from happening.

As a result, we have countless Christian fathers who are nice, kind, involved providers who are spiritually passive, and who have abdicated their Great Commission calling to bring up their children in the training and instruction of the Lord. This was a perfect description of me as a father before God brought me to place of repentance. One of the subtle ways the enemy pulls us away from our primary life-mission of passing faith to our kids is to get us over-involved at church. This was his primary strategy with me. As the lead pastor for our men's ministry, I frequently had conversations with men who were in crisis. We would meet for coffee to talk about their problems and pray together. It was an honor to come alongside these men to offer Christian support and encouragement. Was it good Christian ministry? Yes. Was it part of what God had called me to do in my role as pastor? Yes. But there came a time when I had to ask myself, When was the last time I had spent an hour with my own son? When had I last taken the time to encourage him and pray with him? When had I given him a whole hour of my time to help him grow in his faith?

Should not my Great Commission calling start with my children? Their souls have been uniquely entrusted to my care. The worst thing I can imagine is arriving safely home to my Father in Heaven without them.

THE RENOVATION OF A FATHER

I am grateful that God brought me to repentance before it was too late. No matter how old your kids are, regardless what type of father you have been, it is never too late to repent and ask God to change you! I do need to give you fair warning. If you choose to go down this path of biblical fatherhood, you will become a counter-culture man. You will be going against the flow of many men around you (perhaps even some in your church), so you had better be sure that you have the stomach for this. Do not put your hand to this plow, if tomorrow you are going to tire from your work and turn back.

God never gives up on us. He never gave up on my father, Bill. The greatest miracle I have ever seen is the transformation of my father. In July 2008, at age ninety, my dad was diagnosed with advance cancer. On the evening of August 10' Dad put his full faith and trust in Jesus Christ for the forgiveness of his sins. The transformation in my father was amazing. I was able to spend three days with him before he died on September 3. It was the best three days we ever had together. God brought complete reconciliation to our relationship, and I cannot wait to spend eternity in Heaven with him.[2] God never gave up pursuing my father, and He will not give up pursuing us.

Change Begins with Confession

Confession is a word that means "to say with" or "to agree with." When we confess, we go to God in prayer and say, "I agree with You. My life is not as it should be. I am not loving, serving, and leading my wife as You call me to. I am not bringing my children up in the training and instruction of the Lord. I confess this to You. I am here to ask You to change me. Turn my heart to my wife. Turn my heart to my children." After making this confession to God, I need to extend my confession to my family as well. I need to confess to my wife that I have not been the husband God created me to be, and that I am asking God to change me. I have to say the same thing to my children. I ask them to forgive my lack of leadership in the home and commit to them that I am seeking God's grace to change.

Change Continues with Action

Start where God's Word tells you to start. Begin taking little steps to pray and read the Bible with your wife and kids. After our next chapter on biblical motherhood, we will focus on practical ways that you can lead family worship in your home and intentionally pass faith and character to your kids.

Change Accelerates with Accountability

In my journey of repentance, I have needed other men around me to keep me on task and to keep my heart returning to God's Word. There are some books and sermons to which I continually return. There are men in my church who meet with me on a regular basis. We encourage each other to give our best to our most important ministry in the world: the discipleship of our families. If you do not have other Christian men in your life who can help you stay focused on putting your family first, consider expressing this need to a pastor at your church. Ask him if he would be willing to help you put together an accountability group. Another way to get help is to look around your church and identify a man who has grown children who are passionate about their faith in Jesus Christ. Find a man who has succeeded in the mission you are trying to embrace! While it may be comforting to find other guys who can relate to your struggles, a real powerhouse accountability partner is a man who has already lived the way you want to live.

QUESTIONS FOR REFLECTION:

1. How mature is your love for your wife? Use 1 Corinthians 13 as your measure. What definition from 1 Corinthians 13 is most present in your love for your wife? What definition needs the most attention?

2. How mature is your service to your wife? Are there some specific areas where God would have you increase your service to her?

3. How mature is your spiritual leadership for your wife? What would be your next step to increase your time in prayer and Scripture reading together?

4. Consider God's instruction for fathers to lead with spiritual training and spiritual instruction. What spiritual practice would God have you increase with your children?

5. Personal renovation begins with repentance. If there are things you need to repent of, write them down here, and pray through the list.

ENDNOTES

[1]Many of these studies are available at www.fatherhood.gov
[2]Hear the whole story of my dad's miraculous conversion at vision200. wordpress.com

CHAPTER 7

A Mother's
Love

A Vision for Biblical Motherhood   by Amy Rienow

I HOPE YOU HAVE BEEN ENCOURAGED and challenged through the first part of this journey toward visionary parenting. Rob has shared with you how God has changed him as a husband and as a father. The Lord has done the same for me in my role as wife and mother. Many years ago I made a promise to God that if He ever wanted me to share with others the things He was teaching me, I would do it, even if it was embarrassing. I do not have it all together, but God has graciously been using His Word to teach me and guide me toward becoming the woman, wife, and mother He created me to be.

WHAT BIBLICAL MOTHERHOOD IS NOT

Before we talk about what biblical motherhood is, we need to get rid of a few myths. First, biblical motherhood is not perfect motherhood. God is not looking for Super Mom. We are not going to be talking about the "I-have-the-perfect-house-and-beautiful-children mom." Nor will we paint a picture of the "see-how-extremely-smart-and-talented-my-children-are mom." Nor will we discuss my personal favorite, the "I-am-the-mother-of-five-but-still-have-the-figure-of-a-seventeen-year-old-and-still-work-out-six-days-a-week mom."

It is easy to laugh at these caricatures, but as mothers they reflect the pressures we often feel. We feel as if we have to be perfect and take responsibility for everything that is not perfect around us. Slowly we begin to believe the lie that we should be able to raise perfect kids. I can remember a time when the kids and I were visiting at my mom's house. One of the kids was misbehaving, and I was becoming increasingly frustrated. I had been too frequently addressing the same behavioral problem. The Holy Spirit spoke to my heart, "Amy, do you know any perfect people?"

"No, Lord."

"Amy, are you perfect?"

"Absolutely not!"

"Is Rob perfect?"

"Again, no."

"Then why do you expect to raise perfect kids?"

It was true. There was a part of me that really did expect them to be perfect. Why was I surprised that my children, who are naturally sinful, continued to sin? I would never have verbalized such an irrational thought, but much of my parenting was driven by this hidden expectation. I envisioned that I could train selfishness out of my children, even as I struggled with selfishness myself. The Lord needed to show me that my children *will* grow into imperfect adults. He has called me to guide them, love them, and walk with them as we grow together toward the image of Christ.

ORDERING OUR LOVES

So if biblical motherhood is not perfect motherhood, then what is it? A biblical mother is a woman who has rightly ordered her loves. We are going to explore what it means first to love God, second (for those who are married) to love our husbands, and third to love our children.

Our First Love: God

Although this may seem backward, I want us to look at a portion of Scripture that shows us the opposite of biblical motherhood. It is found in 2 Kings 17:27–33. In this passage, God shows what happens when we mix faith in God with idols of our own making.

> *Then the king of Assyria gave this order: "Have one of the priests you took captive from Samaria go back to live there and teach the people what the god of the land requires." So one of the priests who*

had been exiled from Samaria came to live in Bethel and taught them how to worship the LORD. *Nevertheless, each national group made its own gods in the several towns where they settled, and set them up in the shrines the people of Samaria had made at the high places. The men from Babylon made Succoth Benoth, the men from Cuthah made Nergal, and the men from Hamath made Ashima; the Avvites made Nibhaz and Tartak, and the Sepharvites burned their children in the fire as sacrifices to Adrammelech and Anammelech, the gods of Sepharvaim. They worshiped the* LORD, *but they also appointed all sorts of their own people to officiate for them as priests in the shrines at the high places. They worshiped the* LORD, *but they also served their own gods in accordance with the customs of the nations from which they had been brought.*

These people became so deceived, that in order to show their devotion to idols of stone they sacrificed their own children in the fire. Because their love was not for the Lord alone, their children suffered.

I first read this passage after Rob and I had a big argument. I do not remember what the argument was about, but he was not responding the way I wanted. He went upstairs and I stayed downstairs to sulk. However, after bringing my emotions and anger to the Lord, He led me to this text. Parents in those times were no different than parents today. What would have possessed a mother to do such a horrible thing? How could a mother be so deceived that she would kill her own child? I was angry at these parents who would do this for a stupid idol.

Then the Lord spoke to my heart. "Amy, you are no better." I was shocked. What on earth did God mean by that? God was trying to tell me that in a sense I, too, had sacrificed my family for my own idols. Suddenly, the argument with Rob came into a completely different light. I realized that I had treated him terribly because I had been serving my own idol of pride. At that time in my life, I cared deeply about the praise of others. If Rob did something that, in my mind, tarnished that praise, I was not pleased.

I sacrificed my children to my idol of pride as well. I occasionally made parenting decisions out of a desire to please others and to earn their good opinions. When I was in public I sometimes handled discipline situations differently, to show others what a good mom I was.

When people would give me advice about my marriage or my parenting, I sometimes followed it just to please them so they would think well of me. I was sacrificing my family to my own idol of pride. That night I wrote this poem through tears:

Sacrificing Isaac

It was hard to imagine tossing babies into the fire.
What kind of mothers could be so cruel?
Were they helpless victims themselves
or willing partners in evil—or both?
How is it possible to lay on the altar someone
we love so much?
I was even appalled at Abraham
for following through on God's command
to lay Isaac on a stone.
But who have I laid on a stone
that I have constructed to my false god?
My son, my daughter, my husband?
Yet, unlike Abraham
I act in disobedience rather than in faith.
How deceived I have been
and how much closer to the Israelites am I?
Adrammelach and Anammelech have held altars in my heart,
and I have bowed down, served, worshipped, and sacrificed,
oh yes, sacrificed innocent victims,
a victim myself and a willing partner in evil.
I am no better; only my sin has a better disguise.
Disguise it no more and bring it to light.
Pour down your mercy once again.
I will not become worthless myself,
but I will obey your ancient Word.
Forgive me, Father, for I have sinned . . .
I have sinned.
And as with Abraham's precious son,
save those whom I have inflicted with fear and pain.
Provide for me the right sacrifice.
I will obey . . .
I will obey.

If God is not our first love, we risk sacrificing the things that matter most. A few years ago, I was talking with a friend who ran a day care center in her home. At that time she was caring for a two-year-old girl and began questioning whether it was in the girl's best interest to be there. She shared her concern with the mother who replied, "Well, I could stay home with her, but I love shopping too much." There are certainly situations where day care is needed to provide financially for the family, but for a love of shopping? That woman may one day look back and see that she sacrificed something she cannot regain.

As parents, it is possible to worship God, yet at the same time to serve our idols, which ultimately invites our children to follow the same path.

> *Even while these people were worshiping the* LORD, *they were serving their idols. To this day their children and grandchildren continue to do as their fathers did.*

> 2 KINGS 17:41

Ask God to search your heart. Is there anything in your life outside of Him that you are counting on for your sense of meaning and significance? Idolatry is trying to meet our deepest needs apart from God. Ask the Lord to show you the things you may have put in His place such as possessions, children, husband, physical fitness, social status, or even food. Thankfully, God invites us to come to Him and confess that our hearts are divided. His forgiveness and power to change us are boundless. A biblical mother is a mother who is passionate about God and desires to keep Him first in her heart. This is the first and most important step toward passing a love for God to our children and grandchildren.

Loving Our Husbands

God is to be our first love. For those who are married, our second love is to be our husbands. There are many passages in the Bible that teach women to make their husbands their top earthly priority. We will focus on Titus 2:3–5:

> *Likewise, teach the older women to be reverent in the way they live, not to be slanderers or addicted to much wine, but to teach what is good. Then they can train the younger women to love their husbands and children.*

Entire books have been written on the principles in this passage and in the verses that follow. Look with me at the first part of verse 4, which says that older women should train younger women to love their husbands and children. Notice the word *train*. Many of us enter into marriage with the belief that loving our husbands will be easy. Here God says that loving our husbands requires training. Therefore, we should not feel guilty that it does not come naturally at times. So how *do* we love our husbands? The Scriptures give us many ways, but three have been particularly significant in my journey as a wife.

Respecting Our Husbands

In Ephesians 5:33, God says, "the wife must respect her husband." Let me first say that respecting your husband never means tolerating physical abuse. It does not mean accepting inappropriate control or perverse behavior in your marriage. It does not mean submitting to an unsafe environment. When a wife respects her husband, she freely shares her thoughts, feelings, and needs.

Respect is not politically correct! God's order for the family—God, father, mother, children—is counter-cultural. When God speaks, Satan distorts. If this is God's order for the family, we would expect to see Satan promoting the exact opposite. Just look at a typical television show. The kids are smarter than the parents. The mom always knows more than the dad. The dad is just lucky to be able to take care of himself, but he cannot even do that very well. Oh, and if there is an animal in the family, it is often the smartest one of all. And what about God? He is nonexistent.

God's order is not simply a matter of authority but also accountability. The father is called to be the head of the household and will therefore give an accounting to God for how he spiritually led his family, including his wife. So while the husband is accountable *to* his wife and *for* his wife, the wife is accountable *to* her husband but not *for* her husband. Our husbands deserve our respect because they carry a greater authority and a greater accountability. I feel the weight of accountability for our children, and as I reflect on this, I feel empathy for my husband's heavier load. Yet God has equipped him for this purpose, not me.

Have you ever had a time in your marriage when you did not feel "in love" with your husband? Have you ever felt like you did not even like him? Most of us would answer, yes. I know that in my fifteen years of marriage, there have been times when I struggled with a lack of positive, loving feelings toward my husband. But when I was in these dark places, I often blamed my lack of passionate love on a shortage of romance. What was my solution? I tried to make my husband more romantic. "Take me out on more dates!" "You don't bring me flowers as much as you used to." Of course, all of these tactics never gave me the warm fuzzy feelings I was looking for in the marriage. Instead, Rob became increasingly discouraged because he could not please me. The solution I needed was Ephesians 5:33, *"a wife must respect her husband."*

When I committed myself to respecting my husband, even when he disappointed me, I found my love for him growing. I found "warm fuzzy feelings" coming back into my marriage. Date nights and flowers are wonderful, but I do not *need* them to have romance in my marriage. Romance returned when respect abounded in my heart.

One thing that makes it hard for us to respect our husbands is the underlying disrespect shown toward men in our culture, even in the church. I attended a Christian event for women in which a funny video clip was played about what the men were doing while their wives were away for the weekend. In the staged scenes, men were loading their kids up with ice cream and Coke; they were glued to the television, and were fumbling around the house completely helpless without their wives. The video was funny, because all humor is rooted in some truth. Yet, as I watched, I wondered if a female counterpart video would be shown on a Christian men's retreat. I do not hear Christian men joking about how lost and helpless their wives are when they are traveling for business. Unfortunately, it is easy, even in the church, to paint a disrespectful picture of men and to laugh about it.

As a mother of two sons, I do not want my boys to grow up thinking they are buffoons. I do not want them to think that girls are smarter than they are. How can my sons grow up to be the leaders of their families if they subtly get the message each day that women are more competent than they are? Unfortunately, we have a crisis in the evangelical church because of a lack of godly male leadership. Yet, as women, we have to take some responsibility for this situation because of our own attitudes.

Recently, I had a conversation with a dear friend who was lamenting that she now sees her seven-year-old daughter treating her father with disrespect. She realized that her daughter had learned it from her. We have become so accustomed to degrading comments made about men, and men making degrading comments about themselves, that we do not realize how pervasive the problem is. I challenge you to keep your eyes open for this attitude in yourself, your husband, and your children—and when you see it to confess it to the Lord.

I can already hear many women crying out, "How am I supposed to respect someone who doesn't behave respectfully? I am not going to be a doormat. I am not going to lie and say that I respect him when I don't!"[1]

We need to go back to the instruction for husbands a few verses earlier in Ephesians 5:25a. It says, "Husbands, love your wives, as Christ loved the church." Consider this question. Do we deserve the unconditional love of Christ? Have we earned His love with our excellent behavior? No. We do not deserve it. Yet, "God demonstrates his own love for us in this: while we were still sinners, Christ died for us" (Romans 5:18). Now wives, here is an uncomfortable question for you. Do you deserve the unconditional love of your husband? A person who deserves unconditional love is a perfect person. Are you a perfect person? I hope you say no. You are not perfect. You sin. You make mistakes. You do things that hurt your husband. You let him down. Yet, what does the God of the universe tell him to do in response to you? God says to your man, "Love your wife, as I loved the church."

Now let us consider the other side of the equation. Does a husband deserve the unconditional respect of his wife? A person who deserves unconditional respect is a perfect person. Your husband is not a perfect person. He sins. He makes mistakes. He demonstrates poor character. Yet, what does the God of the universe ask wives to do in response to husbands who do not deserve respect? *Respect them.* God's plan for marriage is mysterious, beautiful, and amazing. He asks men to love their wives even though they do not deserve it. He asks women to respect their husbands even though they do not deserve it. Why would God design marriage this way? Because He knows that He made men and women differently. We have different needs and we respond to different things. When a man is respected, he shows more love to his wife.

When a wife is loved, she shows more respect to her husband. When a husband receives that increased respect, he wants to show more love to his wife. When the wife receives the additional love from her husband, she respects him even more.

Helping Our Husbands

In Genesis 2, God tells us how He created the first husband and wife. God created Adam and then,

> The LORD God said, "It is not good for the man to be alone. I will make a helper suitable for him."

GENESIS 2:18

God provides us with two powerful words here that help us understand the role of the wife in the marriage relationship. Some Christians do not like to talk about this verse, because the world loves to attack us here. "See! See! The Bible teaches that men are better than women, and that wives are less important than their husbands. You Christians think that women are reduced to *helpers*."

This word *helper* is not a word meaning subservience or secondary importance. In fact, there is another Being in the Scriptures who receives this same name: the Holy Spirit of God! (Psalm 118:7; Hebrews 13:6) If the word *helper* refers to God, then we know it cannot be a word that communicates insignificance.

I want to draw your attention to another word in this passage, *suitable*. Out of all God's creation, you can help your husband in a way that no one else can. This is a very encouraging thought. It is amazing to consider that even in the dysfunctional parts of our personalities we are *suitable* helpers for our husbands.

Here is a lighthearted example. When Rob and I were first married, we had a difficult time keeping our new home neat and clean. We were very busy and our home was often messy. On a scale of messiness, with one being extremely neat and ten being a slob, I would have ranked a seven and Rob a nine. Our best friends were on the complete other end of the scale. I marveled at how fastidious they were about their home, their car, even the glove compartment of their car! In a conversation over dinner, I remember saying, "If either Rob or I were neat, we might

A Mother's Love | 87

have a fighting chance at this." Our friend had a great reply, "If one of you was super neat, and the other one was not, you would drive each other insane!" Because I have had to work diligently to become more neat and organized, I am a suitable helper for Rob in this area. I did not like the fact that I was "organizationally challenged," but God perfectly matched me to a man who needed help to grow in this area. When you are discouraged about your imperfections and your struggles, remember that God says you are a *suitable* helper for your husband.

Just because the word used for helper is also used for God the Holy Spirit, it does not mean that we are to be the Holy Spirit for our husbands. Have you ever tried to play Holy Spirit? How is this working for you? When I have done this in the past (and unfortunately still do it in the present) I have found that it usually results in Rob feeling defeated rather than helped. We are not helping our husbands when we inform them of all the things they are doing wrong. We need to be able to confront our husbands in love, but that is different than keeping a running checklist of their faults. I encourage you to pray for discernment that God will show you the difference between nagging and loving confrontation.

Appreciating Our Husbands

Our husbands need to hear "thank you," and they need to feel our gratitude. Growing up in the 1970s and 1980s, I was exposed to a lot of feminist thinking. I was talking with my grandmother several years ago about her years with my grandpa. She said something that really made me think. She said, "I was always thankful to have a roof over my head." I was taken aback at this. I was ashamed to admit to myself that not only had I never told my husband that I was thankful for the roof over my head, but I had not even *thought* of being thankful for it!

Our husbands love it when we appreciate them. Is your husband a hard worker? If so, when was the last time you told him that you appreciate his desire to work hard and provide for the family? Does your husband spend time with the kids and show up at their activities? Tell him you appreciate it. Say, "There are a lot of men in the world who don't give their kids the time of day. You aren't like that. I notice how you make them a priority. Thank you."

Some women are afraid to express appreciation to their husbands because they think that it will make them complacent. The opposite is usually true. A man who feels affirmed and appreciated by his wife is a happy man! Happy men make better husbands and fathers.

The Blessing of a Good Marriage

You might find it odd that in this chapter on motherhood we have spent so much time on how to love God and love our husbands. I am convinced that if we truly give the best of our hearts to God and to our husbands, we will bless our children with a wonderful gift. My home is the training ground for the future marriages of my children. I want to pass a love for God into those marriages. I try to remember that how I treat my husband may be replicated in the homes of my children and grandchildren.

Loving Our Children

As we have already learned, the Bible is the best manual on parenting. Do you want to know how to love your children? Look at how God loves you in the Scriptures and do your best to model it. Do not be intimidated. God is not asking you to be perfect. He invites us to follow His lead, walk in His grace, and gently lead our children toward Him. Here are a few powerful pictures of how God parents us that can inspire us as moms.

God's Love Is Sacrificial

As a mother, you already know that sacrifice is part of the gig. This begins with the nine months of sacrificing your body and the ongoing sacrifice of sleep. Mothers must sacrifice time, money, and many of our personal interests and hobbies. God gave up His Son. There was no greater sacrifice than this. I know there is a fear and concern with moms today that we are so sacrificial we do not care for our own needs. Indeed, this can be a real problem. My concern, however, is how our culture invites us to respond. The message on the talk shows about "mom burnout" seems to be that you need to do more to pamper yourself. "You need more time for you." "You need more time with your girlfriends!" I do not want to overstate this because I believe we do need to be intentional about caring for our physical and emotional health and nurturing supportive friendships. There is nothing wrong with seeking to build downtime, exercise, and time with girlfriends into your schedule. But remember the ordering of our loves: God, husband, kids. As mothers, we must expect to sacrifice. Our job is all-encompassing, challenging, and just plain hard work.

Yet, when we have rightly ordered our loves, over-sacrificing is not a concern. You cannot out give God. He will give us great returns for our sacrifices. Returns such as children who respect us, enjoy being with us, and have a desire to follow us. These returns are worth our sacrifices.

It is when our loves are out of order that we risk burning out. If I put my children ahead of Rob and ahead of the Lord in my heart, then the risk of "losing myself" is very high. The end result would be that my children will take and take . . . and never give back. Children who grow up in the number one place in their parent's hearts often become bitter and resentful. It can create an atmosphere of entitlement in the home. A mom in this position will often feel that she is responsible for making everyone happy, all the time.

Sacrifice is part of what it means to be a mother. The question is, who are you sacrificing for? As a mom, I want to please God even more than I want to please my children.

God Is Slow to Anger; He Is Patient and Gentle

In my walk with God, He has been very gentle with me. But I often wonder how well I am passing that same gentleness on to my children. Many times I have heard myself and the women around me say light-heartedly, "Well, it was one of those mornings . . . I was yelling at the kids all the way to school." I feel that women have a tendency to trivialize this. Many of us say, "I am just not a patient person." So that settles it! No one can expect me to be calm and gentle with my kids because "I am just not a patient person." I have not yet found the Scripture that says, "Raising kids is really hard; God understands, and He does not expect you to be patient." It is not in the Bible. (Believe me, I have looked for it!) Instead we read this in Galatians 5:22–23:

> The fruit of the Spirit is love, joy, peace, patience, kindness, goodness, faithfulness, gentleness, and self-control.

If we lack patience and gentleness, it is *not* okay. It is not something that we can give ourselves a pass on. When we see impatience, the solution is not to accept it, but to repent and ask the Lord to produce the fruit of patience in our character. This is not a one-time prayer or an overnight process. It is a battle. I repent a lot . . . to God, to my husband, and to my kids. When we are struggling with character problems, let us admit it. Do not call them personality traits. When we are honest about our character problems and confess them to the Lord, He increasingly transforms us.

God Longs to Be with Us

How often we mothers exclaim, "I need a break from these kids!" There is absolutely nothing wrong with needing time away from your responsibilities as a mother. Sometimes God makes you take a break. After giving birth to JD, my third child, my body crashed. I was not able to give everything I wanted to Rob and the kids because I desperately needed rest. It was healthy and right for the family to rally around me and to help me through that time.

However, there is a subtle distortion that can creep into our hearts. There is a difference between needing a break from our *work* as a mother versus communicating the message to our children that we need a break from *them*. There is a world of difference between these two. We want to be careful not to relay to our children that we do not want to be around them, or that we cannot handle being with them. Does God ever want a break from you? The Lord has programmed your child's heart with a deep desire to be with you (which the world seeks to rob from them). Do we secretly celebrate when the school year starts? Do we think that the last day of school is black Friday because it means the kids are coming home? Imagine a child overhearing these thoughts. What does it do to the hearts of sons or daughters when a mom regularly looks forward to being apart from them?

It was not until I was in my thirties that I realized that my parents had given me the incredible gift of wanting to be with me. I am sure there were times when my mom was tired and fed up with my attitude, but I always remember her wanting me around. She looked forward to my days off and to the summer in order to have more time to spend with all of us. When I took a trip or went to summer camp, she was happy for me to have the experiences, but also wanted me to know that she would miss me. I wish I had understood as I was growing up what a great gift she was giving me.

The vision here is not to have your kids attached to your hip for twenty years! Rather, it is to have our children know that we desire to be with them so they will become increasingly secure in our love. Then they are more likely to trust us with their hearts and follow where we lead. Do you want the hearts of your children to be with you? Do you want them to share their fears, loves, triumphs, and tragedies with you? Begin by asking God to give you a heart like His—one that desires to be with His children.

God Is a Loving Authority Over Us

You may own your own company, but in the grand scheme of things you are not your own boss. God is the loving authority over us; and if we are married, our husbands also have loving authority over us. God calls us as moms to exercise loving authority over our children. Every mom knows what it is like to give instructions and to receive grumbles and complaints in return. We often reply to this by saying things such as, "I just can't teach my own daughter." "My son responds better to his teachers than he does to me." I went through a time when I was struggling with similar thoughts. My friend Debbie was mentoring me on some parenting issues, and I told her about these feelings. She responded with great wisdom. She said, holding her hand flat at eye level, "Mother is here." Then lowering her hand to chest level, she said, "Teacher is here." The point here is not to minimize the authority of teachers or coaches, but to emphasize the greater authority of the parent! If your kids will not receive instruction from you, there is a heart problem that needs to be addressed. The fifth commandment says "honor your father and your mother." The world encourages our children to give more honor to those outside the home than to those inside the home. The world encourages them to treat their friends well, but tries to convince them that being rude to their siblings is normal. In the same way, it is expected that kids will listen to and obey their teachers, but having a bad attitude with parents is just part of life.

Central to my mission as a mother is to do all in my power to help my children choose to put themselves under God's authority. I do not tell them they can be anything they want to be. Instead, I want them to know that their lives belong to God and they can be anything *He* wants them to be. As Rob will talk about in a later chapter on discipline, we ask our children to submit to us, who they can see, in hopes that they will increasingly learn to submit to God, who they cannot see.

AN ENCOURAGEMENT

Many of us were not raised with a strong calling to motherhood. We were the generation of women who were told that we could be whatever we wanted to be. We were told that the roles of wife and mother would simply fit in with the *higher* aspirations of our lives. It was not until Laynie, our fourth child, was born that I clearly saw this in my own heart. During the pregnancy I found myself saying things like, "After I have the baby my life will get started again." In my mind, my life was on hold during the months of pregnancy and caring for an infant. I felt this way because so many of my priorities seemed to be put on hold during that time. A few months after Laynie was born, she was sleeping peacefully in my arms and once again the Lord whispered to my heart, "Amy, what more *life* do you want than this?"

When God calls you to be a mother, it is a calling into *life*. God has called you to bring a new life into the world. It is a noble calling and a blessing. While we may have many other opportunities and responsibilities, we need not search for more *life* than this!

QUESTIONS FOR REFLECTION:

1. Why do you think that society has such a negative reaction to the concept of wife as "helper" of her husband as described in Genesis?

2. If you are married, pray now and ask God to show you the unique ways that you have been created to help the husband He has given you.

3. Do you feel that you are treating your husband the way that you would like your sons to be treated by their future wives? Do you feel that you are treating your husband the way that you want your daughters to treat their future husbands?

4. Read Galatians 5:22. Which fruit of the Spirit are most evident in you as a mother? Which are least evident? Chose one that is least evident and pray for the next thirty days for God to develop this fruit in you.

5. How do you feel about your calling to motherhood? Do you see it as noble or a burden? Ask God to give you a vision for the noble calling of motherhood.

ENDNOTE

[1] I recommend *Love and Respect* by Dr. Emerson Eggerich. I have drawn from his helpful ideas in that book for the text in this chapter.

CHAPTER 8

The Power
Center

A Vision for Family Worship

WHEN YOU WERE GROWING UP, did your family regularly sit down to-gether to read the Bible, sing, and pray together? If you answered no, you are not alone. In fact, you are in the huge majority. Through surveys at our Visionary Parenting conferences, I have found that only 15 percent of today's parents grew up in homes where they had some type of family worship. That leaves the other 85 percent of us with little or no idea what we are even talking about.

Intentionally spending spiritual time together as a family has histori-cally been called "family worship." Family worship is fun, meaningful, and (believe it or not) can be one of the most eagerly anticipated times of the week for your kids. Unfortunately, family worship is often viewed as synonymous with boring. What we will discover in this chapter is that family worship is the engine that powers the spiritual life of the home. It is the first specific instruction that God gave following the Great Com-mandment in Deuteronomy 6:5–7a.

> *Love the LORD your God with all your heart and with all your soul and with all your strength. These commandments that I give you today are to be upon your hearts. Impress them on your children. Talk about them when you sit at home.*

In verse 5, God gives us the big-picture purpose of our lives: to love Him with our whole being. In verse 7, He takes that abstract, big-picture purpose and gives us a practical, daily action step: *sit at home and talk about spiritual things together.* Worship God as a family in your home! Imagine what wonderful things would happen if your family regularly explored the amazing stories of the Bible together. Think how deeply your hearts would be connected if you talked with the Creator of the universe through family prayer. Would you enjoy being a family that is filled with encouragement for one another to grow in faith and character? All these things happen through family worship.

God has instructed us to prioritize this time into our schedule so that we might pass our faith to our children. In Psalm 78:5–7 we learn more about God's call for faith to be passed from one generation to the next:

> *He decreed statutes for Jacob and established the law in Israel, which he commanded our forefathers to teach their children, so the next generation would know them, even the children yet to be born, and they in turn would tell their children. Then they would put their trust in God and would not forget his deeds but would keep his commands.*

Within this Psalm we find a vision of the power of multigenerational faithfulness. God calls me to impress the hearts of my children with a love for God and to teach them God's Word, so they and their children will know and love God! Then my grandchildren (who have yet to be born) will in turn tell their children. God desires that generation after generation of Rienows will "put their trust in God," will "not forget his deeds," and will "keep his commands."

We have a flawed tendency to think that the way we practice Christianity today is the way it has always been practiced. Many Christian families today act as though the church (Sunday school, youth group, etc.) is primarily responsible for helping their children grow in faith. We fail to realize that Sunday school and youth groups did not exist until the late 1800s. For the first nineteen centuries of Christianity it was understood that parents were called by God to disciple their children, and that the home was the primary place for this to happen. During the twentieth century, Christians began to reflect more closely the secular culture and adopted the model of delegation parenting. Do you want your kids to learn to play the piano? Get them a tutor. Do you want them to learn basketball? Find them a coach. Do you want them to learn about Jesus? Find a good youth pastor. We constantly hear the message that it is not our job as parents to teach and train our children. Our job is to drive the minivan and drop them off with the various professionals who will do it for us. While there is nothing wrong with using outside resources to help us raise our children, when we choose to delegate the responsibility of spiritual training the results can be disastrous.

In a previous chapter on biblical fatherhood, we looked at Ephesians 6:4: "Fathers, do not exasperate your children; instead, bring them up in the training and instruction of the Lord." Family worship is a time of tremendous influence, especially for fathers and grandfathers, because training and instruction come together. It is a time of sharing in the spiritual exercises of the Christian faith as well as an opportunity for teaching and instruction.

FAMILY WORSHIP IN THE EARLY CHURCH

Family worship was the teaching and practice of early Christians. They believed that the worship of God began in their homes. In fact, for the first decades of the early church, there were no Christian church buildings at all.

If a person felt called to be a pastor in a church, he had to demonstrate to the church that he was actively leading and teaching his children to love the Lord. It was a résumé essential.[1] Early Christians believed that each household should be like a small church, and that the head of the household was to be its spiritual shepherd. The home was to be a place of worship, spiritual life, and service.[2]

FAMILY WORSHIP AND THE REFORMATION

During the Dark Ages and Middle Ages, literacy declined, and people were not encouraged to read the Bible for themselves. However, with the invention of the printing press in the 1400s, and the translation of the Bible into common languages, family worship was revived.

In 1556 John Knox wrote, "You must [share with] your children in reading Scripture, exhorting, and in prayers, which I believe should be done in every house once a day, at least."[3]

The Puritans, who were the spiritual founders of America, were totally committed to the practice of family worship. One of the primary responsibilities of church leaders in the 1600s was to visit each family in the community and to assess whether or not the parents were training their children spiritually through the regular practice of family worship.

In 1640, Christians in Scotland published the *Directory for Family*

Worship in which they wrote:

> *The assembly requires and appoints ministers to make diligent search and inquiry, whether there be among them a family or families which neglect the duty of family worship. If such a family is found, the head of the family is to be admonished privately to amend his fault; and in case of his continuing therein, he is to be gravely and sadly reproved by the session; after which reproof, if he is found still to neglect family worship, let him be, for his obstinacy in such an offense, suspended and debarred from the Lord's supper, until he amend.*

Family worship was a major issue of church discipline. Why did these churches take it so seriously? Why did they invest so much time, going from home to home to encourage and ensure that family worship was taking place? Family worship was a top priority because they were passionate about the Great Commission. They wanted, more than anything, to see the gospel of Christ advance locally and globally. They knew that the Great Commission to make disciples began with the souls of their sons and daughters. They knew God had spoken clearly in the Bible that parents and grandparents were to take the lead in the spiritual training of their children and grandchildren. For them, a church could not be serious about the Great Commission if it was not serious about family worship.

Jonathan Edwards frequently taught on the biblical doctrines of family life. In 1751, in his "Farewell Sermon," he wrote:

> *"We have had great disputes [about] how the church ought to be regulated; and indeed the subject of these disputes was of great importance: but the due regulation of your families is of no less, and, in some respects, of much greater importance. Every Christian family ought to be as it were a little church, consecrated to Christ, and wholly influenced and governed by his rules. And family education and order are some of the chief means of grace. If these fail, all other means are likely to prove ineffectual. If these are duly maintained, all the means of grace will be likely to prosper and be successful."*

Edwards knew what continues to be true today. When a young person grows up in a godly home, the chances are very high that he or she will grow up to love God and will arrive safely home in Heaven. When a young person is raised in a home apart from Christ or in a hypocritical Christian home, the chances are slim that he or she will come to Christ and live for Him.

Matthew Henry, in 1704, delivered his "Sermon Concerning Family Religion." He said:

"The pious and zealous endeavors of ministers for the reformation of manners, and the suppression of vice and profaneness, are the joy and encouragement of all good people in the land, and a happy indication, that God hath yet mercy in store for us. Now I know not anything that will contribute more to the furtherance of this good work than the bringing of family religion into practice and reputation. Here the reformation must begin. Other methods may check the disease we complain of, but this, if it might universally obtain, would cure it."

Henry regularly preached the connection between the global impact of Christians and family discipleship. He echoed the truth of the Scriptures that spiritually vital families are central to God's plan to bring the Good News of Christ to the ends of the earth.

FAMILY WORSHIP IN MODERN TIMES

In the late 1800s, our nation moved from an agricultural society to an industrial society. Rather than working near the home as a part of the family business, men moved away from home to work in factories. Kids also left home more than ever before as public schools were built. In the 1900s, women increasingly began to work outside the home as well. All these factors resulted in the cry we frequently hear from families today, "No one is ever home!"

Charles Spurgeon was writing and preaching in the late 1800s when the steep decline in family worship began. In his article, "The Kind of Revival We Need," he wrote:

"We deeply want a revival of family religion. The Christian family was the bulwark of godliness in the days of the puritans, but in these evil times hundreds of families of so-called Christians have no family worship, no restraint upon growing sons, and no wholesome instruction or discipline. How can we hope to see the kingdom of our Lord advance

when His own disciples do not teach His gospel to their own children? Oh, Christian men and women, be thorough in what you do and know and teach! Let your families be trained in the fear of God and be yourselves 'holiness unto the Lord'; so shall you stand like a rock amid the surging waves of error and ungodliness which rage around us."

Spurgeon's message is desperately needed today! Godly men and women in growing churches receive the constant call to get involved in ministry. What this call mean is you should volunteer to help with the programs at church. It is a grave mistake to think of ministry only as something that we do outside our homes. Rather, home is where God invites us to begin the life of faith.

Family worship is rare in Christian homes today. The Scriptures and Christian history call us to rediscover it. In the remainder of this chapter, we will explore some of the key principles of family worship and some practical ways that your family can begin to include this powerful time in your home.

PRINCIPLES OF FAMILY WORSHIP

1: Family Worship Is the Intersection of a Right Relationship with God and a Right Relationship with Family

I want everyone in my family to be growing in their love relationship with God. We Rienows are far from perfect, but by God's grace we are growing. In the same way, I want all our relationships within the family to be healthy, close, and loving. Again, we have plenty of arguments and problems, but God continues to help us. When we gather together for family worship, we seek to be right vertically (with God) and horizontally (with one another).

2: Family Worship Is the Foundation for Worship in Church

If children do not regularly experience worship in their homes, how can we expect them to feel comfortable in church on Sunday morning? Without family worship as a catalyst, worship in church on Sunday can be a rather bizarre hour of their week. All of a sudden they are expected to sit, listen, sing, follow along in their Bibles, and turn their hearts to spiritual things. The reason many children cannot sit still in church services has nothing to do with a so-called short attention span. It is most often a lack of training. When kids consistently participate in family worship in the home, on Sunday mornings parents are able to say to them, "This morning we are going to worship with our BIG family!" I am not saying that practicing family worship is a guarantee your child will love church. Rather, worship on Sundays will not feel weird to them, and you will be laying the best foundation for a lifetime of worship in the local church.

3: Family Worship Will Be a Key Target of the Enemy

Because sitting together in your home and talking about spiritual things is one of God's central callings for your family, Satan will do everything he can to prevent it from happening. You will be attacked by feelings of inadequacy: "I can't teach the Bible. I can't lead spiritual discussions. I don't even have my own act together." Satan will throw crazy schedules at you. Be prepared to have your kids cry and whine at the exact wrong times.

However, I can promise you that if you persevere in making family worship a priority in your home, God will equip you and empower you to do this. God never calls us to do something and then abandons us when we seek to be obedient. Family worship has been at the heart of Christian homes for centuries. How would your family change and grow if you spent more time together turning your hearts to the things of God? God calls us to family worship because it draws us closer to Him, keeps us close with one another, and prepares our children to make a difference in the world for Christ.

THE PRACTICE OF FAMILY WORSHIP

Set a Reasonable Goal

My desire is to get to the point where I have a time of family worship every day. This would be in addition to prayers before meals and before bedtime. The schedule that I establish for our family teaches the hearts of my children what is really important. Our schedule reveals our priorities. So, if we do not have time for family worship because we are always running from one sports practice to the other, what does that teach our kids about what we value? My goal is to set aside time every day for family worship. I am not there yet, but I strive to reach that goal.

Some people will come away from reading this book and, by the grace of God they will be inspired to begin family worship. They will make the big announcement to the family, "Starting tomorrow, we will all meet in the living room at 6 a.m. for an hour of family worship, and we are never going to miss a day for as long as we live!" I love this type of passion, but you know what is going to happen? Tomorrow, the family will get out of bed at 5:59 a.m. and will do their best to hang in there during the family worship time. The next day a few people will be late; things will not go as well as they did the first day . . . and with that the commitment to family worship will be over.

The commitment to family worship must not be a flash in the pan. God wants us to slowly and steadily build this foundation of family worship into our lives. That means we may have to start small. Set a reasonable goal that you know you can accomplish. Simply set your goal for *more* than you are doing now. If this will be a new adventure for you, the goal could be one family worship time each month. If you are currently having a spiritual time as a family once a week, set your goal for twice a week.

Once you decide how often you will have family worship, try and write the dates and times on the calendar. I know what happens when I say I am going to do something when I have time. That is code for, "I am probably never going to do this." This is why I suggest that you write your family worship schedule down and post it on the fridge. Protect that time just as you would an important meeting or game.

Mix It Up

Here are some key elements you can mix and match together to keep your family worship times fresh. Do not feel as if you need to do all of these each time you worship together or that you need to do them in a particular order.

Reading and Responding to the Bible

This can be a simple time where one member of the family reads a few paragraphs from the Bible. Perhaps you have never read the Bible on your own. Family Bible reading will be a great place to start your own journey. I encourage you to begin with the book of Mark in the New Testament. It is an action-packed account of the life of Jesus that will provide opportunities for great discussions with your family.

In my family we tend to read through one book from the Bible at a time rather than jump around from book to book each time we read. After you read the Scripture passage, ask if anyone has any questions. Little children may not know what a particular word means. Others may have questions of curiosity. Your kids may ask questions you do not know how to answer. Do not panic. There is a great response for this, "I don't know, but I'll try to find out." The purpose of reading the Bible together as a family is not to demonstrate that you know everything but to point your family toward the One who actually does.

Invite family members to respond from their hearts to what they hear. It is important for the adults to set the example with this. For instance, we recently read a part of the story of Jacob and Esau in the book of Genesis. The character trait of jealousy was a major cause of the problems in that family. After we read the Scriptures for the day, I shared about some jealous feelings that I was having toward someone in my life, and I asked the family to pray that God would give me contentment. I did not start with, "So kids, can you share a time when you felt jealous?" I shared my own experience first. When we, as parents, respond with humility to God's Word, particularly in confessing sin, we model the needed spirit for family worship.

Some parents feel they need to wait until their children are older before beginning family worship. They frequently say things to me like, "We are going to start family devotions when our kids get into elementary school so they can really understand what is going on." If you have young children, please do not wait to start family worship! If your first baby is in the womb as you read this book, you can start praying and reading the Bible aloud now. Do you have an infant? Put your baby on your lap and read your Bible out loud for a few minutes every day. Give your toddler a few toys to play with on the floor and read the Bible aloud. I think of it as a Bible "spa" for little ones. God's words fill the air, and His power works on their hearts even when we cannot see it.

Little ones will absorb and comprehend a lot more biblical truth than you think. When my son JD was in kindergarten we had been talking about the Ten Commandments in family worship. He learned that it was wrong to take the Lord's name in vain. One day when he was out playing with his friends, he came inside discouraged. He plopped himself down on the couch. We asked, "What's wrong, JD?" He replied, "One of my friends just said, 'Oh my, G–O . . .'" There was an awkward pause. He finished by saying, "And I think we *all* know what the last letter is." It was difficult to keep a straight face. We praised him for remembering the commandment and instructed him how to be a good friend in this situation.

The most common question I get about family worship is, "Can you recommend a good curriculum?" Here are three great resources that can keep your Bible time rich and engaging:

1. *The Child's Story Bible* by Catherine F. Vos is a thoroughly compelling, theologically meaningful walk through the major events in the Bible.

2. *The Big Picture Story Bible* by David Helm and Gail Schoonmaker is great for teaching preschoolers and early-elementary students about God's grand plan to save the world from sin.

3. *Balancing the Sword, Volumes 1 and 2* by Alan B. Wolfe provides questions for thoughtful family discussion from every chapter in the Bible.

However, there is no curriculum that will transform your heart and the hearts of your children. There is no curriculum that will convict you of sin and point you to righteousness. Those things happen through the power of God's Word and the working of the Holy Spirit. Here is what your kids most need during family worship: *they need you to open up the Bible.* They need you to read to them with the conviction that it is the very Word of God and that you believe it with all your heart. This is the ultimate family worship curriculum.

Praying for One Another

If you want to create a home that is saturated with the presence of God, pray frequently together. Do you pray together before your meals? If not, this is a great place to start adding prayer to your family life. Encourage different people to pray each meal, and try to not rush through your prayer just to get to the food. This is another important time of modeling the right attitude toward God in prayer. When it is your turn to pray before eating, take it seriously. Your kids will learn a lot about how to relate to God from the tone of voice you use when you pray. While you may have a traditional prayer that you say before family meals, be careful that a traditional prayer does not become routine or is spoken without conviction.

Praying together as a family before bedtime is a meaningful way to end your day. This time can be hectic, and you may be eager to have all the kids in bed so you can take care of things around the house. Remember, one of the four power moments is right before your children go to sleep. Sit with them on their beds, encourage them to pray, and then you pray. I know many teenagers and their parents who look forward to this time each night because it has always been a part of their relationship. If you have teens and you have never done this sort of thing, do not be afraid to try it. It will be awkward at first, but what could be more important?

Another way to build prayer into the life of your family is to share prayer requests with each other. At the breakfast table, go around the table and ask each person to share something for which he or she would like prayer. Have each person pray for the person on his or her right, offering the request to God. At the end of the day, be sure to get a report from each person on how God answered. Consider getting a small white board where family prayer requests can be written down. This will help keep your family prayer-life visible throughout the day.

Our family enjoys a prayer activity that we call high–low. It is a great way to get the family to talk and to prepare for a time of prayer together. We begin by asking if anyone would like to share the high point of his day, the best thing that happened to him that day. After the first person shares, we invite others who would like to share to give their high points as well. After these high points have been shared, we ask for one person to volunteer to pray and thank God for the positive things we have heard. After the prayer, we shift to the low points. We ask if anyone would be willing to share the low point of her day. Frequently, Amy or I will share first to set the tone of openness. After the first person shares the low point of the day, everyone else has a chance to share their low points as well. Finally, we ask for someone to pray about the low points: the worries, hurts, and concerns that were just shared.

Singing Together

Do not be afraid to sing worship songs together as a family. You might find it helpful to use a worship DVD, a hymnal, or a praise CD. Give different family members the opportunity to choose the songs that you will sing. Little kids may also enjoy using their toy instruments. If you have older kids who know how to play musical instruments, invite them to use their gifts to help the family worship God through song.

I realize that the thought of singing as a part of family worship time makes a lot of people squeamish. It could certainly make me uncomfortable because I do not have musical gifts. But I know how valuable a time of sharing songs can be for the family so I set aside my natural hesitation for the sake of my family. Those of you with teenagers are imagining their negative reaction when you tell them that you would like to sing some worship songs as a family. If you have teens and you do not have a history of family worship together, inviting them to sing with you may not be the best idea at first. It may take time for them to get over their embarrassment. However, if you begin the practice of singing as a family when your kids are young, you will be richly blessed with teens who enjoy singing with you, and eventually grandchildren who will enjoy it as well.

Experiences and Object Lessons

Family worship is not supposed to be dull and boring! Creating fun, memorable experiences helps everyone in the family look forward to family worship and get the most out of it. Putting time and energy into creative games and object lessons is worth the effort. Thankfully, there are people who have already done a lot of this creative work for us. Below I share three fun ideas from Family Time Training (www.famtime. com) that we have used with our kids. [4]

1. Running the Race for God. Before your family worship time, set up a racecourse around the outside of the house. If the weather is lousy, you can do this inside the house by designating one room as the starting line. Instruct the kids that they are to run from that room to another room on the other side of the house and back again. Find a watch with a second hand and give each of the kids a chance to run the racecourse a few times to achieve their fastest time possible. Keep track of their best time.

After everyone has had a couple of turns running the course, bring out a box of winter clothes. Have the kids put on as many layers of winter clothes as they can. Oversized snowsuits and big boots are particularly effective! Once they are loaded up with the winter clothing, have them run the racecourse again. They will have a great time stumbling their way through it. (If you are doing it indoors, be sure that grandma's vintage china is far away from the course.) Because of all the clothes they are wearing, it will take them longer to finish the race. After they have had the chance to achieve their best running time in the winter clothing ask them to change back into their normal clothes and gather the family together.

Open your Bible to Hebrews 12 and read verses 1–2:

> *Therefore, since we are surrounded by such a great cloud of witnesses, let us throw off everything that hinders and the sin that so easily entangles, and let us run with perseverance the race marked out for us. Let us fix our eyes on Jesus, the author and perfecter of our faith.*

After reading, you can explain the experience in this way. "Kids, I hope you had a good time with the racecourse. The reason that we did that was so we could remember the lesson from Hebrews 12. God has a plan for each one of our lives. That is like the racecourse that we set up for you. He wants you to follow His path for your lives. He wants you to run hard for Him. But just as the winter clothes slowed you down in our race, there is something that will slow you down in running for God. In the verse that I just read, what does it say slows us down and tangles us up when we try to run for God? It is sin. When we choose to disobey God, we become entangled in our sin and we fall off the course. God brought us together as a family so we could help each other avoid sin, and run fast for God. If we want to run for God, and get rid of sin, we have to fix our eyes on Jesus. Let's do that right now by praying together and confessing our sins to God, and asking Him to help us to run for Him." At this point, it is best for mom or dad to take the lead in confessing sin. Our kids need to see and hear us doing what we are asking them to do.

2. The Quicksand. We shared another activity with a group of families at our house. We gathered all the kids on a tile area at the bottom of our stairs. There were seventeen kids, ranging from age two to ten, packed into a small area. We then said to them, "Do any of you know what quicksand is?" Some of the older ones raised their hands and informed the group. "Yes, that's right. Quicksand is very dangerous stuff, and the tile that you are sitting on IS quicksand! Your mission is to get to safety, and the only safe place is at the top of the stairs where some of the parents are. You have to find a way to get up there. There are a couple of rules. First, you can't touch the stairs. Second, you can't touch the railings on the stairs. You have five minutes to figure this out. Go!"

At this point, the kids' eyes are all wide with panic. For two minutes they were batting around ideas for how to save themselves from the dreaded quicksand. Then, one boy stood up and called up to his dad, "Dad, come get me!" His father walked down the stairs, picked him up, brought him to the top of the stairs and set him down safe and sound. The other kids all looked at each other and realized it had worked. All the kids then stood up and called for their dads to come down and get them. I was tired after going down and up four times to rescue each of my children.

After everyone had been saved, all the families sat down together and we opened the Bible to read Psalm 40:1–2:

I waited patiently for the LORD*; he turned to me and heard my cry. He lifted me out of the slimy pit, out of the mud and mire; he set my feet on a rock and gave me a firm place to stand.*

One of the parents then said, "Kids, the reason we did this quicksand game was to help you remember something very important. There was only one way to get to the top of the stairs and out of the quicksand, and that was to ask your parent to come down and save you. Similarly, there is only one way for any of us to be saved and go to Heaven. If we want God to save us from our sin, then we have to cry out for Him, and ask

Him to save us. That is why He sent His Son, Jesus; to rescue us from our sin, and to bring us safely home to Heaven."

Activities like these can create memorable experiences that bring the truth of the Scriptures to life.

3. The Power of the Spirit. For this object lesson, you will need an empty, glass milk jug, matches, a letter-sized piece of paper, and a few hard-boiled eggs. Put the milk jug on the counter and lay out the peeled hard-boiled eggs. Place one of the eggs on top of the opening to the milk jug. It will not fit through the hole. Tell the kids, "This milk jug represents you and me. These eggs represent the good things that God wants in our hearts. One of the things that God wants inside our hearts is patience. Can you think of other things that God wants us to have in our hearts?"

"The problem with our experiment is the eggs won't fit through the hole. In the same way, the good things that God wants in our hearts, like patience, kindness, and courage, are not already inside of us. So how can we get these important things that God wants into our hearts?"

Take the piece of paper and roll it up as tightly as you can. (Wooden barbeque skewer sticks also work well.) It will need to be able to fit down the hole and into the jug. Take a match (adults only please), hold the roll of paper vertically, and light the top end of the paper. Quickly drop the paper into the jug and place an egg on top of the hole. The fire will cause a vacuum to form inside the jug and the egg will be sucked in! The crowd will be so amazed, they will want to do it a few more times.

Gather the family together and read Galatians 5:22–23a:

> *The fruit of the Spirit is love, joy, peace, patience, kindness, goodness, faithfulness, gentleness, and self-control.*

Continue with this explanation. "Here are nine character traits that God wants inside of each of us. None of them come naturally to us. The Bible doesn't say that these things are the fruit of people. Rather, it says they are the fruit of the Spirit. This means if we want these things in our hearts, we need God's Holy Spirit to bring them in. Just as we needed fire inside the jug in order to "pull" the egg inside, we need the fire of the Holy Spirit in our hearts, to give us love, joy, and peace. Which of these nine things do you want most for God to bring into your life?" After discussing this question, encourage each person to pray and ask God to bring that character trait into his or her heart.

4. Bible Charades. If you have preschool and elementary-age children, playing Bible charades can be a great learning experience for them during family worship. Invite the kids, either alone or with their siblings, to act out a story or character from the Bible and have the rest of the family guess what or who it is. When my son JD was a toddler, he had particular gift for *dying*. If a charade role required a tragic death, he would jump at the chance to do it. His death as Goliath was particularly memorable. Be prepared for your kids to ask you to join in.

Catechism

Catechism sounds even scarier than singing worship songs. Few Christians today know what a catechism is, and even fewer were raised in homes where it was practiced. While the word is unusual, the practice is simple. A catechism is a series of questions and answers about the Christian faith. The questions are designed to instruct a person systematically in the core truths of the Bible. Catechisms have often been used in Christian education, either in schools or churches, to help students memorize important Bible passages and Christian beliefs. Sound boring? To the contrary! Families who practice this with fun and encouragement will find learning a catechism together one of the most rewarding parts of their family discipleship.

In our home, we use a catechism from *Truth and Grace Memory Book #1*.[5] There are 140 questions and answers we are trying to memorize together as a family. We are up to question 35. The kids sometimes fight over who gets to be the catechizer—the person who gets to ask the questions of the rest of the family. If you could hear my five-year-old, Laynie, answering her older brother's encouraging questions, you would want to start using a catechism in your home! Listen in to the first five questions:

"Laynie, who made you?"

"God made me."

"What else did God make?"

"God made me and all things."

"Laynie, why did God make you and all things?"

"For His own glory."

"How can you glorify God?"

"By loving Him and doing what He commands."

"Laynie, why should you glorify God?"

"Because He made me and takes care of me."

Not only is this child's catechism helping our family memorize key doctrines of the Christian faith, it has also given us a shared challenge and a way to encourage each other as we learn.

FAMILY WORSHIP WITH TEENAGERS

A friend of mine recently tried to lead family worship for the first time. His girls are in their teens. Needless to say, he was not sure how they would respond. After forty-five minutes of great discussion and some prayer, his teenage daughter said, "Dad, why did we wait so long to do this?" It is never too late!

If you begin family worship when your kids are young, moving into the teen years will not be so difficult. However, if you are starting with older kids here are some principles that will help you to be successful.

First, tell them you believe you have not providing something that is extremely important to the family. Tell them you are sorry you have not set aside time for the family to talk about spiritual things. Show the family what it says in Deuteronomy 6. Tell them you would like to start doing your best to follow what God says by beginning to have some times of family worship.

Second, invite your teens into the planning and leadership of the worship time. Tell them you do not want this time be boring or irrelevant to them, and you need their help. Invite them to choose the Scriptures that you read. Ask them to design the prayer time. Give them the freedom to choose some of the worship songs. Part of the motivation for this is to help your teens feel a sense of ownership for what is happening. It will also train them to lead family worship in their own homes someday.

Third, do not be discouraged. Starting family worship with teens may be an uphill climb. They may not feel comfortable opening up about their spiritual lives to you. Be patient with them, and with yourself.

Consider the initial goal for your family of one, twenty-minute worship time each week. In many ways, the teen years are when our kids need us the most. Seeking to connect your hearts in family worship will be worth the effort, and I believe the day will come when your teenagers will thank you for it.

A FAMILY WORSHIP ROOM

We have names for the different rooms in our home. We have a dining room because eating is important. We have bedrooms because sleeping is important. We may have a television room, because . . . well . . . never mind that. When we bought our first home, there was a particular room that was filled with bookshelves. We put our books in this room, and we put a television in there as well. What would we call this room? After talking with the kids about it, they settled on calling it the library because that would identify the room with the value we wanted to elevate, reading books.

With this in mind, we decided to create a family worship room in our home. In the middle of this room is our prayer table. Some people might look at our prayer table and think it is merely a $49 coffee table from Wal-Mart (which it is), but we call it our prayer table. When our family prays together, we often get on our knees around this table. Also in our family worship room, are two large, cushy pieces of furniture so we can sit comfortably during family worship. Most people would call these couches or sofas. Most people call this room in their home the living room or the family room. We have chosen to refer to it as the family worship room because family worship is the most important thing that happens in that room.

FAMILY WORSHIP—THE WHOLE PACKAGE

I have suggested five elements for family worship that can be mixed and matched to fit your schedule: Bible reading, prayer, singing, creative experiences, and catechism.[6]

One of the best traditions that you could begin in your home would be a weekly family worship time when you purposefully incorporate all five elements. Believe it or not, you can do them all in about thirty minutes. Families who practice all five elements on a weekly basis often feel that it is the best part of their week together.

Do not get overwhelmed by all this. Start small. Start somewhere. If you set your heart to the mission God has given you to impress the hearts of your children with a love for Him, then He will give you all the strength, time, and creativity that you need.

QUESTIONS FOR REFLECTION:

1. Did you experience family worship in the home you grew up in? If so, write down some thoughts that describe the experience.

2. Why do you think that family worship is practiced so little in modern culture?

3. How do you think our churches would be different if our church leaders held families accountable for family worship and the spiritual training of their children?

4. What is a practical next step for beginning or increasing family worship in your home? Remember the encouragement to "start somewhere."

ENDNOTES

[1] Book II, section III of The Apostolic Constitutions

[2] John Chrysostom (AD 347–407), Homily 36 on First Corinthians

[3] John Knox, *Letter of Wholesome Counsel* addressed to his Brethren in Scotland (1556)

[4] Family Time Training is dedicated to inspiring and equipping parents to lead fun spiritual training in the home. I encourage you to visit the website where you will find lots of creative ideas and encouragement.

[5] Tom Ascol, *Truth and Grace Memory Book #1* (Cape Coral: Founders Press, 2000).

[6] For more equipping on how to begin family worship in your home, I encourage you to read *Family Driven Faith*, by Voddie Baucham (Wheaton: Crossway Books, 2007).

CHAPTER 9

Discipline
That Disciples

A Vision for Biblical Discipleship

H E DID IT . . . *again*. He broke curfew. He hit his sister. He lied. Now what?

Survey any group of parents to find out what they struggle with and one thing will rise to the top of the list: discipline. One reason for this is discipline, or correction at some level, is an everyday occurrence. However, it is not simply the frequency of discipline that makes it hard for parents. Our struggles with discipline begin with the flaws in our own characters.

If we struggle with laziness, it will be tested. When the same argument between the siblings happens for the tenth time that day, we can easily say, "What's the point? Why should I bother trying to deal with this again?"

If we have an impatient spirit, it will be revealed as we discipline our children. We will toss out snappy, thoughtless consequences just to get it over with. Do we have a short temper? It will be plain when the kids misbehave. A small infraction will result in a big blowup. Our out-of-proportion response will have little to do with the child's behavior but much to do with our poor response to the challenge of discipline.

Are we prideful? If so, when our child embarrasses us in public our main concern will be how this situation reflects on the family or on us as a parent. That may sound noble, but it is really pride. Then, instead of providing loving discipline that helps our child grow and develop, we end up scolding him in anger.

DISCIPLINE = DISCIPLESHIP

The root of the word *discipline* is *disciple*. Discipline is something God commands parents to do for the purpose of forming their children into disciples. The word *disciple* means "devoted follower." Therefore, the purpose of biblical discipline is to help your children become devoted followers of Jesus Christ.

> *For these commands are a lamp, this teaching is a light, and the corrections of discipline are the way to life.*
>
> PROVERBS 6:23

The corrections of discipline are "the way to life" for your child. Notice that the word *corrections* is plural, teaching us that godly discipline takes many forms. Why is discipline the way to life? Because biblical discipline is focused on helping your child become a disciple of Christ.

Proverbs 19:18 puts it this way, "Discipline your son, for in that there is hope; do not be a willing party to his death." If we do not discipline our kids in a godly way, we contribute to their spiritual death. Failing to discipline is failing to disciple.

God's plan for your children is to learn obedience and submission to loving parents they can see, so they are ready to learn obedience and submission to a loving God they cannot see. Ultimately, we are seeking to transfer obedience in our children from us to God. Our goal is that when they leave our homes, they will hold themselves under God's authority and under His word. We want them to do this eagerly and willingly. Our call to our children is, "Follow me, as I follow Jesus, so that you will follow Jesus."

Change Your Vocabulary

The dictionary defines discipline as follows:

1) control obtained by enforcing compliance or order

2) a systematic method to obtain obedience

If we apply these definitions to parenting, we will think that the sole purpose of discipline is to get those kids in line! This is the way most people understand and apply discipline. Their goal is to change the behavior. They want bad behavior to stop and good behavior to start. If only it were that simple.

The biblical call to discipline is far more important and much more difficult. Every single discipline situation you face is an opportunity to lead your child toward being a more devoted follower of Jesus Christ.

Amy and I have tried to change our vocabulary. (We do not always succeed!) When we have an issue that we have to address with one (or all) of the kids, we no longer say, "Honey, we have a *discipline* situation that needs to be dealt with." Rather we say, "We have a *discipleship* situation." Changing the vocabulary in this way can change the entire tone of your response. When you see bad behavior or a lack of obedience, do not think *discipline*, think *discipleship*. Consider how you can use that situation to draw your son or daughter closer to Christ.

The Goal of the Heart

The ultimate goal of discipline is to impress the heart of the child. Everything a child does is made up of two components. These two things can be expressed in different ways:

- behavior and attitude
- actions and heart
- fruit and root

Worldly discipline cares primarily about the behavior. As long as the child cleans her room and does a reasonable job, she can grumble and complain about it all she wants. But as Christian parents, we need to consider our key Scripture in Deuteronomy 6, which calls us back to the priority of the heart. "Love the Lord your God with all your heart, with all your soul, and with all your strength. These commands that I give to you today are to be upon your hearts. Impress them on your children." The ultimate goal of godly discipline is to impress your child's heart. The correction of the outward behavior may be the starting point of discipline, but it must not be the ending point. If your child punches his brother in the mouth, something in his heart caused him to do it! If your child is using drugs and alcohol, there is a *reason* in his heart for doing it.

If our discipline (discipleship) does not reach into the heart of the child, we are all but guaranteeing ourselves long-term behavioral problems. Consider this purely hypothetical scenario. Let us imagine for a moment that due to your rigorous, consistent, and effective system of consequences and punishments your children always behave properly. (I told you it was hypothetical.)

This sounds great, doesn't it? But consider this question. *Why* are your kids so well behaved? They are totally obedient because they want nothing to do with the punishments that will come their way if they are not. What will happen to these angelic teenagers when they head off to work or college, where the threat of those consequences can no longer reach them? There are two possibilities. The first is that with their new-found freedom they will break every rule they can find. The other option is that they will live like Pharisees. They will continue to follow all the rules and be proud of it. They will be content to be clean on the outside, even though their hearts are far from God.

If we do not reject the world's version of discipline and embrace a biblical view of discipline that is ultimately focused on reaching the hearts of our children, we are preparing them for rebellion or legalism. Biblical discipline must address both the negative behavior and the reason for the negative behavior, the what and the why. Biblical discipline considers both the negative choice and the feelings and thoughts that came together to create that choice.

A Bad Example

One of the reasons I love the Bible is that it is filled with struggling parents, just like me. We all need the grace of God if we are going to make it through! In 1 Kings chapter 1, we are given personal insight into King David's relationship with one of his sons. In particular, we are told about David's approach to discipline.

The context for this passage is that King David is about to die, and he has declared that his son Solomon will inherit his throne. However, his son Adonijah wants to rule and is prepared to overthrow his father by force.

> *Now Adonijah, whose mother was Haggith, put himself forward and said, "I will be king." So he got chariots and horses ready, with fifty men to run ahead of him. (His father had never interfered with him by asking, "Why do you behave as you do?")*

> 1 Kings 1:5–6

David was a man of great success in many areas, but it appears that disciplining his children was not one of them. In this passage we find that he failed to consider both the *what* and the *why*. First, David failed to interfere with his son. He failed to assert himself and redirect Adonijah's choices. The word *interfere* can carry a negative connotation. No one likes to be interfered with. However, part of biblical discipline is interfering in the wrong choices your kids may want to make. This is not a call to be a nuisance to your kids, but rather a call to intentionally block them from making destructive choices.

David failed to get involved with the *what* of Adonijah's life and the *why* as well. This passage presents a marvelous parenting question, a question that reaches to the heart. "Why do you behave as you do?" David had never asked Adonijah that question! If your son cheats on his test, ask him "*Why* did you cheat son?" If your daughter gossips about a friend, ask her, "*Why* did you spread those rumors about your friend?" The choices your kids make come from their hearts. Wise parents consider not only the action but the reason for the action: "Above all else, guard your heart, for it is the wellspring of life" (Proverbs 4:23).

Heart Rebellion

Most of the time when we need to discipline, we are confronted with both an incorrect action and an incorrect attitude: a wrong choice and a wrong heart. Sometimes, however, we encounter a right action with a wrong attitude. For example, suppose you tell your son to apologize to his sister for calling her a name. He says "Sorry!" in a whining, insincere tone of voice. He was obedient. He said he was sorry. But did he mean it? Was his attitude right? No way. Or, suppose your daughter calls from her friend's house. She asks to come home past curfew. You say, "No." She shouts, "Fine!" and hangs up the phone. She comes home on time but grumbles all the way to her room. In these situations there is outward obedience or compliance but inward resentment and hostility. There is heart rebellion.

If discipline is ultimately about the heart, we cannot let these situations pass by. If we fail to address a problem of the heart when we see it, we are training the child to be a Pharisee. Look at these situations of inner rebellion (where the problem is not the behavior but the attitude) as great parenting opportunities. These are prime moments to go directly to matters of the heart, without the complication of disciplining outward behavior. It is less a moment for discipline and more a time for discussion. There is no need to run interference on bad behavior. You can get right to the heart question, "Tell me, why do you feel this way right now?"

There is another great danger with ignoring moments of heart rebellion. These situations, if ignored, can brew deep anger in our hearts toward our kids. Heart rebellion grates on us and interferes in our relationships with our children. If we do not address these heart issues, our irritation and anger grow. Then when an outward act of disobedience happens, we blow our stacks! If you find that you tend to race from zero to sixty on the anger scale when your kids do something wrong, perhaps you have not been dealing with their heart rebellion along the way. I find that when I discipline with inappropriate anger, it is often because I have ignored a series of heart-rebellion issues.

So what might this look like in real life? Suppose you ask your son to clean the kitchen after dinner. He mutters, "Fine, I'll do it." He then proceeds to sulk and complain while he cleans. Do not miss your chance to gently say, "Hey, son, let's take a break. Come over here on the couch with me for a minute. It's okay. You're not in trouble. I just want to talk with you. I appreciate the fact that you are willing to clean the kitchen, but I can see that things on the inside are not going well. Can you tell me how you are feeling? What is making you upset?" Dive right into the matter of the heart. When we see a bad attitude, we are seeing a crack open up to the child's inner self, to his heart. Follow that anger to its source. Follow that sadness to its root. This is a critical skill of wise discipleship.

If you have lost a heart connection with your children, you may need to make multiple attempts to have open discussions with them before they will respond honestly to your questions. Keep in mind, they may not know the answers themselves. But do not let that discourage you from trying to communicate with them. Keep knocking at the doors of their hearts through these moments of heart rebellion.

DISCIPLINE THAT DISCIPLES IS CONSISTENT

I imagine that every one of you has heard this before: discipline that disciples is consistent. If you pick up 100 books on parenting, you will find this principle 100 times. So our problem, when it comes to consistent parenting, is not so much a lack of knowledge but a lack of execution! The heart of this principle is that children thrive in the context of structure and predictability. They like schedules. Following a plan helps them relax.

Here are three guaranteed results of inconsistent parenting. (These come straight from my vast personal repertoire of parenting mistakes.)

1. Inconsistency Trains Children to Be Professional Whiners

Day 1: We are in the checkout line at the grocery store.

Kids: "Dad, can we get some candy?"

Me: "No, kids, not today."

Kids (ramped up): "But, Dad! Come on!"

Me (calmly): "No, kids, not today."

Kids (pleading): "Just a piece of gum?"

Me (in control): "Sorry, guys, the answer is no."

Pretty impressive, huh? Just wait.

Day 2: We are back in the checkout line at the grocery store.

Kids: "Dad, can we get some candy?"

Me: "No, kids, not today."

Kids (whining): "You never get us candy!"

Me (frustrated): "Okay, you can pick some candy."

I have just trained my children to whine using one of the most powerful psychological tools known to man. The tool is called random reinforcement. This has been tested on people as well as on animals. When I was in college, I was given the assignment to do psychological research on random reinforcement with a rat. (Not exactly the most pleasant work.)

Our rat was named Nebuchadnezzar. Our goal was to get the rat to push a lever as many times a possible. In the first study, every time the rat pushed the lever he received a pellet of food. This is called direct reinforcement: one push, one pellet. With this setup the rat pushed the bar many times a day. In the second study, the rat had to push the bar twenty times in order to get one pellet of food. This is called interval reinforcement. Nebuchadnezzar pushed the bar many more times each day in this scenario compared to direct reinforcement. Lastly, we experimented with random reinforcement. The food pellet was provided at random, after two pushes or perhaps after one thousand and two pushes. In this scenario my little friend became a bar-pushing machine! If the rat was awake, it was pushing the bar. Nebuchadnezzar did not know when the next food would come, so he just kept pushing the bar.

Gambling casinos use this same principle. Gambling thrives because of random reinforcement. The slot machine is the ultimate example. I am sad to admit it, but I am often the parental version of the slot machine. Most of the time, when the kids whine, they do not get what they want. Most of the time, I win. But sometimes . . . at *random* times . . . I cannot take their whining anymore, and I give in.

So what will my kids do when they get random reinforcement for whining? Whine some more! Push, push, push! The truth is, the fault is not entirely theirs. I trained them to do this, and I used one of the most powerful tools in the psychological arsenal to do it.

How do we avoid creating this pattern of random reinforcement? We must think carefully about every yes and every no before we say them. In Matthew 5:37a, Jesus said, "Let your 'Yes' be 'Yes,' and your 'No' be 'No.'" If I am in the checkout line, and the kids ask for gum, before I answer I need to think, "Is this a good time for them to have gum or not?" (Yes, I am one of those terrible parents who occasionally allow their children to have gum .) If it is an appropriate time, I get to give them an immediate, "Yes!" If it is not, a simple, "No, not today" will suffice. Make your choice, and stick with it. If you have been a model of inconsistency up to this point, it will take some time of letting your yes be yes, and your no be no before your kids adjust.

2. Inconsistency Trains Children that They Can Break Any Rule More than Once

Here are some common parenting phrases and approaches that train kids to keep breaking the rules.

The Repeated Direction

Suppose that your son is playing a video game. You politely inform him that it is time for him to start his homework. "Okay," he replies. Five minutes go by, and you return to see him still playing the game. "I thought I asked you to start your homework!" you respond. Another five minutes pass, and the game is still on. Now you are angry. "If I have to ask you one more time to do your homework, there is going to be a consequence!" Lo and behold, your son gets up and the homework begins. By repeating your instructions (and increasing the volume each time), you have trained your child that it is okay to ignore your simple requests and instructions. He has learned he only needs to obey you when you get angry.

The Window for Continued Disobedience

I did this a lot when I first had kids. I gave an instruction: "Put that down and come over here!" Then I started counting: "One . . . two . . . three!" There is a reason parents of small children use this one-two-three method to coerce obedience. It works! Many times, a toddler will sense you are getting serious, and she has learned that a consequence will come once her parent says the dreaded, "three." But this method can actually train your child that she can disobey you until the last possible moment. You have seen it happen. "Put that down." No response. "Come over here." Nothing but a glare. "One . . . two . . ." Still nothing. "Thr . . ." Quickly the child puts down the toy and comes to you, just before the ". . . ee!"

The Empty Threat

Imagine a trip where you have been driving several hundred miles and the noise from the back seat is getting louder and louder. You issue a threat: "If you don't change your attitude right now, we are turning this car around and canceling this vacation!" Have you ever issued a threat to your children that you really did not mean? We use these tactics as parents, because when we are at our wits end, these dramatic threats can bring immediate results. The downside is that while you may get a temporary break in the action, you are creating long-term problems. Nuclear threats will actually train your kids to be bolder in their disobedience the next time, because they will know there is a good chance that, once again, you will be all bark and no bite.

We should be very careful when we say, "If you do that, then here is what is going to happen to you." When we are unwilling or unable to bring the consequence that we promise, we erode our own authority. Our kids may end up saying, "Mom and Dad don't do what they say, so why do I have to?"

A few chapters ago we looked at Ephesians 6:4. "Fathers do not exasperate your children." Few things exasperate and rouse deep anger in the hearts of our kids like inconsistency.

So what is the solution to these common problems? When your children do not obey the *first* time that you ask them to, or if they break a rule, you should quickly and calmly deliver an appropriate consequence.

Suppose you say to your daughter, "Please come and do your homework now." A few minutes later the video game is still on. She is not responding to what you have asked. Quickly and calmly say to her, "I'm sorry you didn't obey me when I asked you to start your homework. As a consequence for this, you have lost your TV time this weekend. It is time to start your homework now."

The If-Then Chart

Are you looking for more consistency in your parenting? Creating an If-Then chart is a great place to start. You can create this simple chart on a piece of paper or poster board.[1] Simply draw a line down the middle of the paper, creating two columns. On the left side, at the top of the page, write, "If." On the right side write, "Then."

Use this chart to decide, in advance, what the consequences will be for various problems that you are dealing with. For example:

IF ...	THEN ...
... you don't do your chores with a good attitude	... you will have to clean an extra bathroom
... you bring inappropriate music into the house	... you lose your CD/MP3 player for a week
... you call your sibling a name	... you get a dab of soap on your tongue
... you get a speeding ticket	... you lose your license for three months
... you complain about your dinner	... you lose your dessert

There are many reasons why this can be a powerful discipleship tool for you and your kids.

- It lets you break out of an angry punt mode. Typically, this is how I feel when the same behavior has happened five times in an hour. I am angry and scrambling desperately to come up with some discipline or response that will deal with this intolerable situation. However, when I use the If-Then chart, I do not have to get upset, and I do not have to think furiously to identify some crazy new consequence. I am able to calmly respond to what happened by saying, "I am sorry that you made that choice. You know what the consequence is for your decision."[2]

- It gives consistency and predictability to your kids. If you do not like being in an angry punt mode, I can assure you your kids like it even less. Knowing consequences in advance will actually help your children make better choices.

- It is flexible. If a consequence is not working, change it! It is helpful to try and choose consequences that are related to the offense. If your son talks back to you (a sin committed with the mouth), you may choose the consequence of a spoonful of vinegar (a consequence to the mouth). If your daughter is rude to her brother (a sin within a relationship), then she is not allowed to spend time with her friends that weekend (a consequence relating to relationships).

- It can be collaborative. This will amaze you. Many families will actually sit down and write out the If-Then chart together. Talk about what the key behavior areas are that need to be worked on. Discuss fair and appropriate consequences together. You may be surprised when your kids suggest stricter punishments that you would!

- It can be used with equal success for rewards and encouragements. It is a great idea to have one section dedicated to consequences, and another section focused on rewards. For instance:

IF ...	THEN ...
... you help your brother with his homework	... you will get to rent a movie over the weekend
... you help clean the kitchen without being asked	... you get extra dessert tomorrow

- It is effective at any age. Consider some illustrations of this tool with a teenager.

IF ...	THEN ...
... you break curfew	... you lose one hour of curfew at your next three social events
... you are disrespectful to Mom or Dad	... you have to clean Mom and Dad's bathroom

Teenagers respond to this because it gives them a sense of control over their lives. If they do not like cleaning Mom and Dad's bathroom, and I imagine they do not, they do not have to do it! They can avoid that task by being respectful instead. It is their choice. If they want to enjoy hanging out with their friends next weekend, they know they will need to be on time this weekend.

BIBLICAL DISCIPLINE INCREASES CONSEQUENCES TO CAUSE CHANGE

Have you ever given a consequence to one of your kids only to have him respond, "Oh, that sounds great! I thought you were really going to punish me." I hate that when it happens to me. Clearly, the choice of consequence was not adequate to deter him. A consequence is not a consequence if it does not cause some pain or discomfort. Kids are not supposed to like discipline. A consequence is not effective if it does not lead to a change in behavior. The solution is to steadily increase the severity of the consequence until you see change in both the actions and the heart.

I have misapplied this principle many times by making the only increase the volume of my voice or my anger. When I ask my kids to do something and they do not do it, I think that if I just yell the instruction again and louder, it will get done. I use my anger and my tone of voice as the consequence for disobedience. There is a consequence, but it is not a consequence that brings change in the behaviors and attitudes of my kids. What really happens in these interactions? I drive the hearts of my kids away from me in an effort to get them to do what I want. Biblical discipline allows a consequence to be the source of appropriate pain for our kids rather than our anger. I am sorry to admit it, but it is a rare week when I do not have to say to one of my kids, "I was harsh with you. That was wrong of me. Will you please forgive me?"

When I resort to anger and yelling, I have left discipleship in the dust. I have short-circuited the process of training the hearts of my children because I am fed up! I just want the problem to disappear as fast as possible.

Do you want an ultimate character test? Try to use a gentle tone of voice with everyone in your family for an entire week, no matter what the situation. Speak gently with your children. Feel free to deliver tough consequences as needed, but do it in a gentle tone. It will stretch you to the limit, and it will also be a giant step forward in building a loving relationship with your kids.

Here is a personal example of how we had to implement increasing consequences in our family. One night when we went out to eat, we were working with our six-year-old daughter, Lissy, on keeping her bottom in her seat when she was eating. She had just received a new pack of gum from me (sadly through random reinforcement!). We were waiting for our meal and she was squirming. So I said, "Lissy, because you are out of your seat, I am taking away a piece of your gum." She briefly protested, and then sat down. A few minutes later she was squirming again. "Lissy, I hate to tell you this, but I am going to take away another piece of gum.

Please stay in your seat." This time her protest was more passionate. She only had three pieces left! Once again, her bottom left her seat, so I took away a third piece of gum. At that, she said, "Dad, no more! I will sit still now!" And she did. I had to continue to ramp up the consequences until the behavior changed.

This principle applies to parenting teens as well. Suppose your teenage son comes home an hour late. You calmly let him know that because he chose to break curfew, next Friday night he will have to be home an hour earlier than usual. Next week rolls around, and he misses the early curfew by ten minutes. This time you say, "I am sorry you came home late again. Because you missed curfew for a second time, you are now grounded next Friday night, and your curfew will be two hours earlier than normal. If you respect that time, then we will be able to begin giving you some of that time back for the following week."

Consequences must continue to increase until behavior changes. I have seen many parents, especially when their children become teenagers, bail out on this principle. Unfortunately for you, Mom and Dad, increasing consequences may require decisions that inconvenience you! You may have to take away your teen's driver's license. Then you will have to drive her to work. You may have to remove your son from a negative school environment, find a new school for him, or begin home-schooling. I bet you have heard your kid, in an effort to have you give in on some issue, say something like, "Mike's parents let him do whatever he wants!" If that is indeed the case, then Mike's parents are among the many who have bailed out. The discipleship of your son or daughter is worth every effort and every inconvenience.

DISCIPLINE THAT DISCIPLES IS CONNECTED TO GOD AND HIS WORD

If we have any hope of reaching the hearts of our kids when we discipline them, our approach must be centered on God and His Word. Here are seven basic steps to demonstrate how discipline that disciples might look.

Suppose you have just discovered that your ten-year-old son stole a video game player from someone at school. You found it in his backpack, and after asking a few leading questions, he confessed that he stole it.

Step 1: Confirm What God Wants from You, the Parent

"Son, what does God say that I need to do as a parent in this situation?" (The response we are looking for from your son is, "You need to discipline me.")

"That's right. Proverbs 19:18 instructs me as your parent to discipline you, for in that there is hope; and if a parent does not discipline, then that parent hates his child. Do I hate you?"

"No, you don't hate me."

"You're right again. I love you, and I need to be obedient to God."

Step 2: Talk About What Happened

"Now, let's talk about what happened. What did you do? Be honest with me and tell me the whole truth." (At this point you are trying to lead your son to confess clearly and completely exactly what he did. This is an essential part of confession and forgiveness.)

Step 3: Turn to the Bible for Wisdom and Correction

"Son, thank you for telling me the truth about what you did. What does God say in the Bible about the choice you made?"

"Well, the Bible says that stealing is wrong."

"That's right. In Exodus 20 we find the ten commandments, and one of those commandments is, "You shall not steal."[3]

Step 4: Focus on the Loving Heart of God

"Son, let me ask you a more difficult question. Why do you think God commands us in the Bible not to steal?" (This may require some conversation, but the goal of this step is to help your son understand that God commands us not to steal because when we steal from others it damages our relationships with them, we hurt innocent people, it is a sign of our lack of trust in God to provide for our needs, etc.)

"Son, God loves you very much. He knows that if you steal, then both you and others will be hurt. That is why He tells you not to steal."

Step 5: Open the Heart

"Son, you have told me what you did. Now can you tell me why you did it? What feelings were inside of you? What was in your heart that led you to do this?" (Your goal here is to create a safe environment where your son can express his feelings of jealousy, boredom, hatred . . .whatever they may be. If you cannot help him discern the motives that led him to steal the game, then you cannot influence his heart. It may be difficult for him to articulate his feelings to you. You might share a time in your life when you stole something and describe the feelings you had.)

If you have not been in the habit of having heart-level discussions with your children, this process will be difficult at first. They will likely be defensive and may even give you the impression they are aggravated with you. It will take many attempts on your part to win their hearts. You must focus relentlessly on this mission to reconnect with the hearts of your children. If you do not have their hearts, then you do not have influence.

Step 6: Calmly Deliver the Consequence

"Because you made this choice to steal this game, here is your consequence. You need to return the game system. You need to save your money and buy a new game for this person as an act of restitution, and you need to personally go to the person's home and apologize to both him and his parents." (Whatever consequence you deliver needs to be given calmly, with a gentle voice. The consequence should be the thing that hurts, not your anger.)

Step 7: Affirm Your Love

"I am sorry that you made this choice. Please remember that God commands me that I have to do everything I can to help you become more like Jesus. I love you very much."

Perhaps you read through these seven steps and are thinking, "Rob, doing discipline this way is going to take a ton of time!" That is the point. Discipline can be quick, but discipleship takes time. The choice is yours. Perhaps you have heard this parenting maxim before: rules without relationship equals rebellion.

One of our favorite parenting phrases comes from Proverbs 23:26. In that verse a father writes to his son and says, *"My son, give me your heart."* If you were to listen to conversations in our home, you would frequently hear Amy or me asking one of our children, "Will you give me your heart?" Do you have the hearts of your children? Do they trust you with their deep feelings and secrets? If so, thank the Lord for this, and make it a daily mission to keep their hearts close to yours. If not, pray fervently for God to bring your hearts together. As you win and keep the hearts of your kids, you are in the position that God wants you to be: not simply disciplining your children but discipling your children.

QUESTIONS FOR REFLECTION:

1. How did your parents discipline you? What was the result?

2. Which of your character flaws are revealed when your children do things wrong?

3. How do you think it would change your discipline if you approached each situation with the attitude that it was a "discipleship opportunity?"

4. Do you see passive rebellion in your children? What is your normal response to it?

5. If you are married, do you believe you and your spouse are on the same page when it comes to "discipleship situations?"

6. If you do not already have an "if-then chart", take the time right now to begin thinking about things you might put on it.

7. How often do you use your anger as a punishment? If you struggle with this, offer a prayer of confession to God and ask Him to change your heart and this character issue in your life.

ENDNOTES

[1] If you don't want to create your own page, consider buying the "If-Then" chart from *www.doorposts.com.*

[2] For more practical ideas for tough discipline situations consider reading *Say Goodbye to Whining, Complaining, and Bad Attitudes . . . In You and Your Kids* by Scott Turansky and Joanne Miller (Colorado Springs: Shaw Books, 2000).

[3] If you are not sure where to find things in the Bible, you can use a website like *www.biblegateway.com* and search the Bible for the subject or word that you are looking for.

CHAPTER 10

To the Ends
of the Earth

A Vision for the Kingdom of God

W E NOW NEED TO EXTEND OUR VISION beyond our family and our children. God did not create the family as an end in itself. God's purposes for your family and for your children reach far beyond the particular life you have together in this time and place.

I believe God wants us to dream big. It is a godly thing to have dreams and visions for a future that only God can accomplish. Imagine a church that is blessed with one thousand people coming to worship each weekend. The members of the church, along with the staff and elders, gather for a weekend of prayer. They plead with God to do a miracle in their church, and they ask the Lord to bring them twenty-five new people in the next ten years to join their church. Huh? They dream of growing by twenty-five people in ten years? That is definitely *not* a God-sized vision. That is not a dream that would require the supernatural intervention of the Creator of the universe. God is not a small-dream God, and He does not call us to be small-dream people.

I am passionate about the church and about the advance of the gospel of Jesus Christ to the remote parts of the earth. I have a dream for family ministry. It is a 200-year dream, which can only come to pass if God works a miracle of His grace.[1]

My dream is to have a Christian training ministry where people receive sixteen to twenty years of intense, personal discipleship. After this time of thorough training in the Scriptures and Christian living, each person would be mentored for the next thirty to fifty years. My dream is that in 200 years, God would use this discipleship plan to shape 78,125 men and women for His purposes. If 1 percent of these followers of Christ were pastors, that would mean 781 pastors were trained, equipped, and released. If .5 percent of these followers of Christ were missionaries, 391 missionaries would have been launched to the remote parts of the earth. I also dream of these Christians giving faithfully of their money to the ministry of their local churches. If each person made an average of $40,000 per year, this would translate into $312 million of giving, every single year. If each person worked for an average of forty years, over $12 billion dollars would be used to advance the cause of Christ around the world.

I told you this was a big dream! This is a vision that cannot be accomplished by human effort. There is little I can do to bring this to pass. It will take a miracle, and that is exactly what I am praying for. But is a dream like this even possible?

Jesus looked at them and said, "With man this is impossible, but with God all things are possible."

MATTHEW 19:26

Earlier I said that this was a dream for our family ministry. When I say *family ministry* I am not talking about the call God has given us at church or through Visionary Parenting. I mean *the Rienow family ministry.* Amy and I are asking God to work a miracle. Here is our prayer.

God, would you work a miracle and lead our five children to know and love you with all their hearts? Would you then give each of our children, on average, five faithful children? Would you then give each of our grandchildren, on average, five faithful children? Would you continue this blessing, generation after generation, for the next 200 years?

If God were to supernaturally answer that prayer, in 200 years Amy and I would have 78,125 descendents living for Christ and bringing the Good News of the gospel to the world.[2] Will all of our children and grandchildren get married and have children? We do not know. God may call some of them to serve Him through singleness, or others to adopt rather than become pregnant. It is not our job to manage the details, but God does want His people to have a multigenerational Kingdom vision!

Consider how the impact changes as the numbers change. If the generational impact number is five, as we see above, in 200 years, God will have blessed the world with 78,125 of our descendants who are followers of Christ. What if it were four? What if we had four children, and each of our children, on average had four children, and this repeated for the next 200 years? With that vision, there would be 16,384 followers of Christ, 164 pastors, 82 missionaries, and $65 million dollars per year in Kingdom giving. What if there were three faithful children per family, generation after generation? In 200 years there would be 2,187 believers. What if each family had an average of two children who were faithful to Christ? In 200 years there would be 128 Christians advancing the gospel in the world. And what if each family had only one child? In 200 years, seven generations from now, there would be just one follower of Christ.

My message here is not that good Christians have lots of kids. Nor am I saying that people are unspiritual or not committed to God if they have no children or have a small family. Rather, I want to help you catch a grand vision for how God wants to use families, parents, grandparents, and children to fill the earth with worship and bring the Good News of Jesus Christ to the ends of the earth.

What if the generational impact number were eight? What impact could the Rienow family ministry have if God blessed us with eight faithful children, and He worked a miracle and blessed each of our children, grandchildren, and beyond with an average of eight faithful children? In 200 years, there would be 2,097,152 people who love Jesus and are sharing the gospel, serving their churches, and impacting their communities. If 1 percent were pastors, that would be 20,972 pastors. If .5 percent were missionaries, that would be 10,486 missionaries. Using the financial numbers we used above, Amy's and my descendents would be giving over $8 billion per year to their local churches, with the total amount given over the 200 years of our family ministry would be more than $383 billion dollars. This is a God-sized dream, and only He can accomplish it.

One of my favorite quotes comes from William Bradford, who led the Pilgrims across the Atlantic on the Mayflower. In his journal, *Of Plymouth Plantation*, he explained the mission that drove them to move their church from Holland to the New World:

We cherish a great hope, and an inward zeal, of laying good foundations for the advance of the Gospel of the Kingdom of Christ to the remote parts of the earth, even if we should be but stepping stones to others in the performance of so great a work.[3]

In our family, we often use this same mission statement to describe the calling that God has given to us.

UNLESS THE LORD BUILDS THE HOUSE

In Psalm 127, God speaks to us about this multigenerational Kingdom dream. It is a poem with just five verses, and yet it is rarely considered or preached as a single unit. Christians either focus on the first part of the Psalm or on the second part, but we should look at it as a whole.

Unless the LORD builds the house, its builders labor in vain. Unless the LORD watches over the city, the watchmen stand guard in vain.

In vain you rise early and stay up late, toiling for food to eat—for he grants sleep to those he loves.

Sons are a heritage from the LORD, children a reward from him.

Like arrows in the hands of a warrior are sons born in one's youth.

Blessed is the man whose quiver is full of them. They will not be put to shame when they contend with their enemies in the gate.

In verse 1 we read, "Unless the LORD builds the house, its builders labor in vain." This is not a generic principle about making sure that you are not living your life and planning your future apart from God. This Psalm is about family and about children. When it says *the house* it means your house, your family. We know this because the psalm quickly proceeds to the issue of the heritage and reward of children.

Children are frequently referred to by people from all different faith systems as a blessing from God. How true this is! Unfortunately, when Amy and I first got married, this was a blessing that we wanted to limit and delay. Engaged couples are frequently asked, "How many, how soon?" In other words, how many children do you want to have and when do you want to start? When people asked us this when we were engaged, we said, "We think we'd like to have three to four kids, and we'll start having them in three years." We had a plan. This area of our lives was completely under our control.

Interestingly, when it came to other major decisions in our lives, we did our best to seek God's will, not ours. Was this the right job to take? We did not just make a list of pros and cons and make the decision that seemed right to us. We prayed. We sought counsel. We turned to the Bible. We wanted to follow God's will, not ours. We sought God's will about where He wanted us to live. We thought we were taking the big decisions of our life before the Lord. We were, except for one of the biggest decisions of all. When it came to "how many, how soon" we never sought the will of God. We did not even realize this was an area of our lives where we were supposed to seek wisdom and direction from Him.

In the Bible, God promises many rewards for those who follow Him. There is a list of some of them in Galatians 5:22–23a:

> The fruit of the Spirit is love, joy, peace, patience, kindness, goodness, faithfulness, gentleness and self-control.

These are nine blessings and character traits the Holy Spirit wants to give us. We do not take credit for these things; they are fruit that the Lord brings out in our lives as we follow Him. There are many other rewards for following God. He blesses us with salvation, forgiveness, hope, and eternal life. Consider each of these rewards for a moment. Are there any rewards or fruit of the Spirit that you do not want? Would you ever say, "God, I'd like all the love, but frankly I could do without the kindness"? No way! We want them all. We want as much of every reward as God will give us. We are right to want all the rewards that come from following God. We want them all, we want them in full measure, and we want them as soon as we can get them. Except for one . . . "*Sons are a heritage from the LORD, children a reward from him.*"

God says children are a reward from Him! Yet, when it came to that reward Amy and I planned to limit it, control it, and delay it. We did not have a multigenerational Kingdom vision! The Psalm goes on to say, "Like arrows in the hands of a warrior are sons born in one's youth. Blessed is the man whose quiver is full of them. They will not be put to shame when they contend with their enemies in the gate."

God has called you to be a parent! He wants you to clearly understand that having children and raising them in the Lord is central to your mission in this life. God's desire is for your children to *launch* from your home someday like arrows into spiritual battle for Christ and His Kingdom! In verse 5, God says that a person with many children is blessed. Do you believe that? The world would say otherwise. The world would say that having many children is a burden, not a blessing. Who do you believe? When you see a large family get out of a fifteen-passenger van, what goes through your mind? I believe that if we had the heart of God we would say, "Wow! God has really blessed them."[4]

A PRAYER TO BEGIN

Are you willing to take the courageous step of inviting God into this area of your life? Are you willing to actively seek His will when it comes to having children? Or will you choose, like Amy and I did, to make all those decisions in your own strength? In the pages of Scripture, God is not silent about the issue of having children. Will you search the Scriptures to see what God has said?

Embracing a new multigenerational vision begins with prayer. Perhaps your journey will begin with a prayer like this:

> *Lord, we open every area of our hearts and lives to You. We do not seek our will for our lives, but Yours. We do not want to do what is right in our own eyes, but in Yours. When it comes to this decision of having children, we want Your will to be done, not ours. Guide us to Your will. Use Your Word. Use the counsel of others who believe Your Word. We believe Your Word when it says, "Unless the LORD builds the house, its builders labor in vain." We ask You to build our family according to Your will and plan for our lives.*

A PRAYER TO CLOSE

The multigenerational journey starts with prayer and dependence upon God, and it continues in the same way. I am grateful that you have taken the time to explore a small part of what it means to become a visionary parent. The world does not need more smart people, more athletic people, more musical people, or more artistic people. Those are all fine things. However, the world needs people who love Jesus Christ more than anything else. God has entrusted the immortal souls of our children into our care so that we might do all in our power to impress their hearts with a love for Him. We are to invite them into God's multi-generational Kingdom mission and, one day, by His grace we will arrive safely Home together.

I encourage you to join me in continually lifting up a prayer like this to God:

> *Dear God, please give us, our church, and our children, an eager Christian love for children. Please work a miracle of grace in our children, grandchildren, and beyond so they will love You more than we have, they will know Your Word better than we do, and they will carry the gospel of Jesus farther than we can. We lift up the souls of our children, our grandchildren, and the generations yet to be born. We ask that every single one of them would put his full faith and trust in Jesus Christ for the forgiveness of his sins. We ask that each of them would make a difference for Christ and His Kingdom, and we ask most of all, that one day, we would all arrive safely Home. We pray these things in the name of Jesus, Amen.*

QUESTIONS FOR REFLECTION:

1. How would our churches and communities change if every family had a God-sized vision for reaching the world for Christ?

2. What can Christian churches do to increasingly teach people that making discipleship, reaching the world, and having children all go together?

3. How have you made your decisions about having children? Has it been an area that you have completely controlled, or a decision that you have eagerly brought to the Lord?

4. If you were to write a mission statement for your family, what would you include?

5. Has God used Visionary Parenting to impact your family? What might the Lord have you do to share the message with others?

ENDNOTES

[1] Thanks to Doug Phillips and Geoffrey Botkin for the challenge to dream a 200-year dream.

[2] That number refers only to the number of men and women in that particular generation. If we included their parents and grandparents who may be still living, the number of faithful descendents alive could be as high as 96,875.

[3] William Bradford, *Of Plymouth Plantation* (Mineola, NY: Dover Publications, 2006).

[4] Would you like to wrestle in a deeper way with these important questions? I encourage you to read *Start Your Family* by Steve and Candace Watters (Chicago: Moody Publishers, 2009).

WOULD YOU LIKE TO SHARE the message of Visionary Parenting with your church family? Visionary Parenting is available in a DVD series, taught by Rob and Amy Rienow. This eight part series is a great way to equip the parents and grandparents in your church to pass faith and character to their kids and grandkids. The DVD series works well in adult classes or small groups.

Live Visionary Parenting Conferences are also available. Hosting a live conference is a powerful way to impact your entire church with a vision for family discipleship.

To get more information about ordering the DVD series or hosting a live conference visit our website at www.VisionaryParenting.com.

PARENTING TEENS
BY RICHARD ROSS AND DAVID BOOTH

PRICE: **$3.99** 13-ISBN: 9780892656011

Parenting Teens is a fully laminated product containing 14 panels of valuable information for parents. Each panel contains valuable content for parents seeking to raise teens to live a life of faith and fellowship with God. Topics discussed include: real success, the role of parents, discipline, church involvement, facing tough issues, praying for your teen, and much more.

- Great quick reference for parents to place in Bible and review often.
- Ideal tool for youth ministers seeking to equip parents.

randall house

To order call **1-800-877-7030** or visit **www.randallhouse.com**

GROUP
DISCOUNT
PRICE:
$8.99
(discount on
carton of 24)

LAUGHING IN THE MIDST OF MARRIAGE
LINDA ANN CROSBY

PRICE: **$10.99** 13-ISBN: 9780892655779

- A reminder for wives to laugh and have fun as they live out every rich, poor, sick, healthy, better, or worse vow.

- 52 short devotionals to help wives place their focus back on God, who is faithful to provide all they need.

To order call **1-800-877-7030**
or visit **www.randallhouse.com**

randall house

It's a LIFE
CURRICULUM!

BY RANDALL HOUSE

D6 Curriculum
connecting church and home

Adult

Young Adult

Teen

Elementary

Preschool

D6family.com